SO-BEZ-893

Model Behavior

MAKE YOUR
CAREER PATH
YOUR CALLING

Model Behavior

MAKE YOUR
CAREER PATH
YOUR CALLING

Amy Robnik Joob

REDEMPTION
PRESS

© 2019 by Amy Joob. All rights reserved.

Published by Redemption Press, PO Box 427, Enumclaw, WA 98022
Toll Free (844) 2REDEEM (273-3336)

Redemption Press is honored to present this title in partnership with the author. The views expressed or implied in this work are those of the author. Redemption Press provides our imprint seal representing design excellence, creative content, and high quality production.

No part of this publication may be reproduced, stored in a retrieval system, or trans-mitted in any way by any means—electronic, mechanical, photocopy, recording, or otherwise—without the prior permission of the copyright holder, except as provided by US copyright law.

Unless otherwise indicated, all Scripture is taken from the Holy Bible, New King James Version®. Copyright © 1982 by Thomas Nelson. Used by permission. All rights reserved.

Scripture marked NIV is taken from the Holy Bible, New International Version®, NIV®. Copyright ©1973, 1978, 1984, 2011 by Biblica, Inc.® Used by permission. All rights reserved world-wide.

Scripture marked NET is taken from the New English Translation, NET Bible®. Copyright ©1996–2006 by Biblical Studies Press, LLC, http://netbible.com. All rights reserved.

Scripture marked NLT is taken from Holy Bible, New Living Translation. Copyright © 1996, 2004, 2015 by Tyndale House Foundation. Used by permission of Tyndale House Publishers, Inc., Carol Stream, Illinois 60188. All rights reserved.

Scripture marked KJV is taken from the King James Version of the Bible, public domain.

ISBN 13: 978-1-68314-783-1
ePub ISBN: 978-1-68314-784-8
Kindle ISBN: 978-1-68314-785-5

Library of Congress Catalog Card Number: 2018963929

What Others
Are Saying

Model Behavior is just that . . . a model for finding your ministry in your work. Joob walks the reader through her discovery and modeling career into how she refined it into her ministry calling. From the glitz and glamour of the modeling industry to becoming the boots on the ground, Amy Joob shows how God works to the good in all things.

—Cindy Sproles, bestselling author and
cofounder of Christian Devotions Ministries

So excited for this book! Amy Joob has always been a joy to work with at MET-Rx and Pure Protein booths. She has always displayed "model behavior" from her work ethic and personality to an example of how to be a positive force no matter what the task at hand.

—Teresa Hartle, senior manager
Grassroots & Sports Marketing, Nature's Bounty Co.

Amy's words capture, inspire, and compel you. I could not stop reading her powerful story of God's faithfulness and provisions. Her writing left me feeling challenged and ready to step into what God has for me. Her faith journey is truly an inspiration!

—Emily Norman, connection pastor,
Willow Creek Community Church, Crystal Lake, Illinois

A fantastic book! Amy gives a rare insight into the modeling world and her soul! I've had the pleasure of hiring her many times, and because of her kind, gentle spirit; her inner and outer beauty; and her professionalism, she has always been my first choice! Kudos to you, Amy!

—Ava Anthony, owner, LIVE Event Productions

Amy Joob was a great influence in launching my career as a Ford model fifteen years ago when I was a new student in Bible college. Amy's beauty and spirit radiated the love of Christ. I observed the wisdom and glowing smile of this modern-day Queen Esther while never compromising her Christian beliefs for the sake of her job. I only hope her story can touch and inspire young women to be strong for Christ.

—Crystelle Tipton, model, Ford Models

In our contemporary world, with a shortage of positive role models, Amy Joob's voice rings true and needs to be heard. Young women searching for wisdom in finding their own unique career paths will find direction and encouragement in *Model Behavior.*

—Becky Melby, author, Guideposts Secrets of Wayfarers Inn Series

Amy has authored a wonderful account of how she has become the "beautiful" woman who has become a friend. While any first impression of Amy will confirm for you that her outer shell has all the makings of a professional model, I first met her at 6:00 a.m. on a running trail for Team World Vision. Her true beauty is far deeper than first impressions. No matter how our outward appearance predicates others' first impressions, what truly shapes us is the journey that forms our vision of the world. I pray that you will take the time to journey with Amy in order to see her purest beauty that only can be shaped in faith-filled living.

—Rev. Lance R. Lackore,
First Congregational Church of Huntley UCC, Illinois

Model Behavior takes the readers on a delightful journey of "blooming where you are," despite your circumstances. The vivid illustrations of experiences, successes, and failures reminds one of a symphonic concerto being played with continual dissonance throughout and then harmonized at the end by the conductor—God, our Sovereign King. If you or your daughter have experienced tragedy, disappointment, or defeat, you must encounter this book. It will encourage you to take one more step toward your happiness, fulfillment, and resolution.

—Dr. Karen C. Love, vice chairman, Love Family Christian Foundation

I have known Amy throughout her modeling career, and she has always been one of my top choices in Chicago. Amy's professionalism, poise, integrity, kindness, and compassion show through on every job, and she has been asked back repeatedly by the same clients. It has been a pleasure to work with Amy, and I know you will see her heart and passion shine through in her book *Model Behavior*. Enjoy!

—Anne O'Briant, Anne O'Briant Agency Inc.

Amy has always been an inspiration by the way she has lived out her faith and her calling. This book is a beautiful reminder of how God has a plan and a purpose designed for each of us. Through *Model Behavior* she reminds us to embrace the imperfections and our uniqueness and allow God to use us where we are called.

—Dave and Natalie Mudd,
pastors at Alpine Chapel in Lake Zurich, Illinois

This book is very encouraging to anyone questioning getting into the modeling industry. Amy walks us through her experience of modeling from the start of knowing nothing to working with large national brands. She shares her apprehension regarding the business, surrounding both her faith and how she viewed herself—for example, her concern regarding her facial birthmark, which she saw as a weakness, and how she was encouraged despite this. She shows that the things we see as flaws can become a trademark that makes one unique and stand out. The business is developing a more open mindset, breaking through the archaic guidelines and gatekeepers. I highly recommend this book to anyone interested in moving forward into the talent market.

—Sarah Anna Hansen, photographer, www.sarahannahansen.com

Ever since I met Amy, I have seen her drive, desire, and determination to become healthy and to better love her family and those around her. Her passion is contagious, and you will be drawn into each story of adventure as you watch in amazement how God works in and through her life. You will find yourself motivated to take next steps toward your own dreams with each page you read. When I think of Amy, I think of Proverbs 12:15. She is a wise woman who takes instruction and is very responsive to God's voice. I think she will motivate you to hear and respond to His voice too. I highly recommend *Model Behavior*!

–Dr. Jill Noble, DC, CFMP, Wellness Nutrition Center

Model Behavior by Amy Robnik Joob offers a warm view of successful possibilities for any young woman desiring to follow her dream-come-true career. Joob shows how she maneuvered through uncertainty yet stayed true to her purpose. Written from her own experiences and soul-searching, this is a fresh and inspiring read that I highly recommend!

–Susan Marlene, author of devotions and short stories

Woven masterfully within her own amazing story, Amy reveals timeless truths with great insight on how our lives can have incredible purpose as we allow our vocations to be our calling! An encouraging read for those with nontraditional callings and unique talents and gifts!

–Phil Baker, founder, MinistryStudiesOnline.com

Amy's life is a great story with an even greater purpose. I've had a front-row seat to Amy's life, faith, family, and career, and she's the real deal through all the ups and downs. Are you ready to go to the next level? Grab a copy of *Model Behavior* and let Amy show you the way.

–Daryl Merrill, lead pastor,
Christian Life Church in Mt. Prospect, Illinois

Amy is a high-energy, super-positive, creative, can-do, live-by-faith-not-by-sight kind of woman. Her writings and now this book are authentically raw and genuinely inspiring. She has had this book in her ever since I met her, and I am so happy that it is happening. She has a way with words, drawing you into the excitement and joy of living outside the box but not outside of God. I love that, and her.

—Karen Schultz, city director Refuge for Women, Chicago

It has been my privilege and joy to have known Amy Joob since her early college days as a student at Christian Life College in 1995. From my earliest observation, Amy has always had a heart to fervently seek after God and to earnestly seek to know and do His will. We have had many opportunities to share meals together and conversation regarding her calling and destiny. Amy has always demonstrated a willingness to listen to counsel, and she seemed comfortable enough to share her heart—seeking Godly wisdom as to whether to proceed toward a career in modeling or as a motivational speaker at high school assemblies. Many high school students' lives have been touched and reached as she authentically shared her life struggles with them. One of Amy's biggest passions has been to write a book and have it published. I am so glad to see that her dream became a reality.

—Jeri Oleksy, secretary and director of women's ministry,
Christian Life Church in Mt. Prospect, Illinois

To Mom, for believing in me and always encouraging me to model.

To Dad, for instilling in me a passion for reading, writing, and books.

To Eric, Arianna, and Ashton, for your laughter, faith, and love, which brought me and this book to life.

Foreword

Ms. Amy Joob is a true inspiration. Her book candidly shares her range of emotions as she pursues her destiny. To take a leap of faith in an industry that seems to strive on the shallow and external, we realize how much faith, commitment, support, perseverance, and hard work actually are the drivers for Ms. Joob's success.

Like many of us, Ms. Joob wears many hats—a wife, mother, daughter, friend, etc. The demands placed on her are enormous. She is able to embark on a new journey and new experiences with grace and style. Because she is grounded in her faith, she is able to be secure in her position in various new environments and shares these experiences in a way that allows us to embrace her story.

As a professional, I have recommended, hired, and worked alongside Ms. Joob. She epitomizes not only what a model should be but what an exemplary employee should be. *Model Behavior* and Amy Joob are synonymous. This book depicts an individual who has looked deep within her purpose and is able to incorporate her true being into her mission and all facets of her life and work.

Although there is a specific demographic targeted, this book can be read by anyone at any age, at any time in one's life. We all hope that our life paths and our career paths are parallel. Ms. Joob shows how, by doing so, there is harmony in our existence. She is a wonderful example on how to ensure that if you are authentic, if you are real, you are able to achieve any goal.

Each chapter encompasses a lesson. Her career and her life's example can be reflected on and used as an example for navigating how and what we want to aspire to and ultimately achieve. If we wind up in an uncomfortable arena, we can look at Ms. Joob's experience. If we put up smoke screens or feel intimidated, we can see what Ms. Joob has done. We can all learn from one another, and Ms. Joob is a teacher who is not intimidating in the least but open, honest, real, and sweet. She truly is a giver in every form of the word, and this *Model Behavior* is a gift that she has given all of us.

Simriti (Simi) Ranajee, PhD, MBA
CEO Centers for Analgesic Transformation
Former Ms. India Worldwide

Acknowledgments

First, I want to thank God for not giving up on me and for revealing His love to me through Jesus Christ when I was twenty-one years old. Without Him, I don't think I would be here today, and my story would not exist.

And a big Minnesota bear hug to my husband, Eric, for your tireless support over the years—from my running, to modeling, to writing, and now to publishing. Thank you for not letting me give up on modeling in the beginning and for your deep pockets, which have funded this book. And to Arianna and Ashton—thank you for making me laugh, for the dance breaks, hugs, creative input, and for all the extra chores you did to help Mom out on this journey.

A special thank you to Mrs. Jerilyn Fortner, my high school English teacher. Thank you for believing in me and shaping me and my writing in those early years. Thank you, Pastor Daryl Merrill, for encouraging me to write my life story while we were at CLC, and to Leslie for praying for me and my family over the years. Thank you to Nicole O'Dell for pushing me out of my comfort zone and giving me my first writing opportunity through Choose Now Ministries.

A huge shout out to Debbie Lykins for everything you have done for me over the years. If it weren't for you, I don't even think this book would be published! Thanks for your guidance, counsel, and ability to make me laugh when I need it most. And to my editor Beth Jusino—thank you for your patience and for all that you taught me about writing throughout the many drafts of this book. Thanks for taking a chance on me! Thank you to Inger Logelin, Athena Dean Holtz, and Hannah McKenzie from Redemption Press for believing in me and walking with me through the publishing process.

A special thank you to the entire Robnik family for your support and for all the refreshing R & R in Minnesota. And to Eric's parents, Fred and Linda, and the Joob family—thank you for supporting us in so many practical ways through this process and helping us with our kiddos so we could work, write, and see this project to completion.

Thank you to all the friends who have encouraged and prayed for me on this journey. Lee Fisher, thank you for your unconditional love, fashion, and health tips and spurring me on to "keep writing"! Janet Reich, thank you for supporting every fundraiser and cause in our family and for the love your family has shown all of us.

Thank you to those who proofread early versions of this book: Stacy Doran, MaryLou Erickson, Fred Joob, and Jan Haggerty—you all deserve a gold medal! Thank you to my Team World Vision texting prayer group—Judi, Linnea, Ella, Clara, Carrie, Terre, Anne, Margarette, and Karen—I appreciate your unconditional love and behind-the-scenes support. And thank you to my CLC friends—Amanda, Sharon, Jac, Heather, and Danielle—for your prayers and much-needed girls' night outs. You helped me keep my sanity! Thank you to my industry friends—Kim, Jen, Patti, Kelly, Farrah, Sia, Melanie, Tanya, Joana, Wendy, Denise, Danette, Starlight, Lisa, and April—for showing me love both at work and outside of work. And to my childhood friends—Stacy, Robyn, Patti, and Carol—thank you for loving me unconditionally and helping to shape me into who I am today. I am thankful for our forty-plus years of friendship! And to Jackie, Stephanie, Veenu, and Lee, thank you for helping me to look beautiful!

A heartfelt thank you to Jeri Oleksy and Renee Ertl, who covered me in prayer, offered me wisdom, and helped me to stay on the right path during my travels and throughout my modeling career. And to Joanne Magoc for your mentoring, wise counsel, and love that helped me to heal. A big shout out to Willow Crystal Lake! Thank you Pastor Marcus Bieschke and especially the 9:00 a.m. Greeters Team—you have been a backbone to our family.

Last but certainly not least, a huge thank-you to the companies, clients, agencies, and production companies who hired me over the years. Without all of you, this story would not be here. I am beyond blessed by the work opportunities you sent my way! Thanks a million to Nature's Bounty/MET-Rx, PCNA (Porsche Cars North America), Q-Center/Accenture, Symphony Bridal, Accent Event Productions, Anne O'Briant Agency, Aria Talent, Chicago Talent Network, Creative Impact Group, Definitive Models and Talent, Emmrich Agency, Event Pros, Holzer and Ridge Casting, Image Model & Talent, Independent Talent Source, Jennifer's Talent, Karen Stavins Enterprises, Lily's Talent, Live Event Productions, Live Marketing, Lori Lins Ltd., Productions Plus, Real Talent, Red Mink Productions, Royal Model Management, Shirley Hamilton Inc., Showmax Marketing, Strut Productions, and Unique Models & Talent.

And to you, the reader—thank you for picking up a copy of this book. I have been praying for you! I hope my story sparks something inside you that will ignite your passion and creativity and that you will take the next step toward your purpose and destiny. Who knows? Maybe I will be holding *your* book in my hands one day soon.

Table of Contents

Introduction

I never planned on a career in modeling.

A vocational interest inventory I took at fifteen stated I was best suited to be a hotel manager, police officer, or firefighter. I thought seriously about being a cosmetologist. And then, during my junior year, I won a spot on the Miller Hill Mall fashion panel in Duluth, and that led to a handful of modeling jobs.

At fifteen, I also landed in some Advanced Placement classes, and that eventually convinced me I could handle higher education. I enrolled in Bethel College at eighteen alongside my best friend, Stacy. I honored my parents' wish that I stay in-state my freshman year, but I couldn't wait to get out and see the world.

Traveling, new experiences, and my desire to gain independence led me to Auburn University in Alabama for my sophomore year. I had a rebellious streak, and I was on a mission to escape personal pain in my life. I was drowning my sorrows in drinking and wild living. My goal was to party hard and die young.

Thankfully, God had another plan.

Despite my crazy lifestyle, I declared a major in criminal justice my sophomore year. Drawn by the excitement of living life on the edge, I decided I wanted to work as a detective for the FBI. My dad, who worked as a computer systems analyst for the US postal service, had sold me on the excellent benefits federal government employees receive.

However, my world turned upside down during my junior year at Auburn. I spent five weeks in Europe earlier that summer. I enjoyed sightseeing in Amsterdam and on the Spanish Riviera. but I also pushed my limits on partying during the course of the trip. God began to open my eyes and show me where my crazy lifestyle could lead, and I felt empty and hopeless.

I was twenty-one, and I hit rock bottom. My friend Annie saw my need and took me to church. There I met Jesus, and for the first time ever, I truly experienced His love and acceptance. In the best decision I have ever made, I accepted the salvation He offered, and I finally found the freedom I'd been looking for.

The trajectory of my life changed dramatically. People began telling me, at church and back home, "God is calling you, Amy. He has a great plan for your life." But I didn't know what that meant. Was I now supposed to enroll in Bible college and become a pastor or missionary or evangelist?

I'd always had a heart for kids and teens, and I'd been volunteering through Project Uplift (like a Big Brothers - Big Sisters program) since I'd arrived at Auburn. Once I gave my heart to Jesus, I wanted to help hurting teens like me. I decided to walk away from my goal of working with the FBI and instead began training to prevent young people from becoming criminals. I stayed in criminal justice but switched from law enforcement to youth services.

I did my internship in law enforcement since I was still torn between that and youth services. In my heart, however, I knew God was steering me in a new direction.

I also began training for triathlons during this time. I threw my energy into running, biking, and swimming—all of which were far healthier than the drinking, smoking, and partying I'd done before.

I graduated from Auburn in 1994 and headed home to Minnesota, praying for direction for this *calling* people were still telling me I had. I learned I didn't need to be a student at the University of Minnesota–Duluth to be a part of the triathlon team there, so I joined. I also volunteered with the youth group at Cloquet Gospel Tabernacle (now Journey Christian Church) and counseled with the youth pastor, Phil Baker, and senior pastor, David Ogren.

Eventually, after much counsel and prayer, I decided to move to Chicago. I was envisioning being a youth pastor in the city, but God led me to Christian Life College in Mt. Prospect, located in the northwest suburbs of Chicago, instead. I was still a new Christian, and I needed to be grounded in my theology. There I met Eric, who would eventually become my husband. I continued to volunteer with a local youth group while earning my degree in pastoral studies.

After I graduated from Christian Life College, I managed a local teen center and continued my triathlon training. I did very well in competition and dreamed of going pro in the sport. And then, two separate accidents brought injuries that set me on different path.

I married Eric at twenty-six, entered modeling school at twenty-seven, and started my professional career at twenty-nine. I felt like I was jumping off a cliff as I began one of the biggest adventures of my life.

Chapter 1

Not Your Average Sunday

*Faith is taking the first step even when you
can't see the whole staircase.*
MARTIN LUTHER KING JR.

I stepped out onto the runway, and the spotlights blinded me. My
feet were crammed into shoes that didn't belong to me and were a size too
small, but I wore a beautiful designer garment, and I was on the arm of one
of the most famous, sought-after hair stylists in the country. According to
his assistant, I had just received a $500 haircut. She had told me that news
backstage as she did my nails and another assistant put on my makeup.

I felt like Esther from the Bible. Just like that unknown girl chosen to
do something great, much to my disbelief, I'd been chosen in an audition.
It was late September 2001, about a month shy of my thirtieth birthday.
My modeling career was taking off, thanks to a boost from Frederic
Fekkai.

I'd started the morning normally, going out to breakfast with my husband, Eric, and then to church. I said to him over pancakes, "I wonder if this is just another cattle call. There'll be so many models from different agencies. Do you think it's even worth it to go to this audition?"

"Hey, it never hurts to try," he reassured me. "If you don't knock on doors, they'll never open."

So after church, I drove downtown for my audition at a high-end hair salon on Michigan Avenue. I stood in line with many tall, thin, young, beautiful women. Knowing that I looked and seemed younger than my age gave me a surge of confidence as I observed the other models around me. I prayed for favor as I waited with these beauties to audition for the celebrity hair stylist.

After interviewing with Frederic and his assistant, I was told to wait to one side of the room with a handful of other models. Once the long line of auditioning hopefuls ended, Frederic's assistant walked over to us. "Ladies, Frederic has chosen you to be models for the hair show. Congratulations."

I was still basking in the glow of being chosen when the assistant started giving instructions. Words I did not expect trickled into my ears, and I realized she wasn't talking about the hair show that started the next day. "Reception . . . Navy Pier . . . cocktail dress . . . benefit . . . runway . . ."

Wait, did this job start *tonight*? My agent had only told me about the Monday show. I'd had a huge pancake breakfast, and my stomach felt bloated. I didn't have any of my modeling gear–shoe bag, makeup kit, or undergarments–in my car. My house was two hours away, and there was no way I could get those items in time for an evening show.

I felt the panic rise. I needed this job. I was helping Eric go back to college, and I was carrying the burden of being the main provider.

When the assistant finished talking and turned to walk away, I pulled my courage around me. I straightened my back, sucked in my tummy, and lifted my chin the way Mrs. Newport taught me in modeling school . . . and then I went and groveled. I explained that I didn't have anything with me to work that night. I started to tell her about how my agent said the show was on Monday, but the assistant interrupted me.

"It's fine. We have things for you. Just be at Navy Pier by five. By the way, can you give Frederic a ride over there?"

Did she just hear me swallow hard? Can I give the world-famous stylist a ride in my filthy 1997 Pontiac Sunfire? I didn't know what to say. If I said yes, I'd die of embarrassment over the condition of the car. If I said no, my lack of flexibility and hospitality could cost me the job.

The assistant must have seen the consternation on my face. "You know, don't worry about it. We can get Frederic over there another way. I think he's just going to hop in a cab."

And just like that, God took care of me again.

The show at Navy Pier that night was a benefit for the firefighters and police officers in New York, as it was just a couple of weeks after 9/11. Uniformed men and women swarmed around the grand ballroom, mingling and sipping drinks as they talked in quiet tones. In the center of the room was the longest runway I had ever seen. It made Simi's runway at Union Station look small.

I was nervous but also excited. I felt blessed to be chosen and to have such a wonderful opportunity, yet I worried that I would not fit into the clothes or the shoes they were providing for me. I kept whispering prayers that everything would turn out okay.

I arrived onsite and was whisked right into the dressing room. The woman there literally turned up her nose at me. Clearly, I did not measure up to her standards. *Oh, well! Frederic picked me, and that's all that matters. You'll have to deal with it. I deserve to be here.*

She handed me my wardrobe and shoes, and one of Frederic's assistants escorted me backstage to get my hair and makeup done. Not only did those ladies make me look fabulous, but they gave me a pep talk as well. "You are so lucky to be his main haircut model."

"What?" I didn't realize that other models weren't all getting a haircut or even a style by him. Frederic Fekkai owned a salon in New York and did hair for many famous people.

God had chosen to grant me favor. That was the only explanation that made sense to me.

When the ladies finished with me, they directed me to Frederic's station. I felt like I was walking on air. I floated over and sat down in his chair. He started to work his magic.

"Could you please part my hair over the left side of my face?" I asked. "I have a birthmark over here, and I always try to cover it with my bangs."

"Sure, no problem. I can do that for you."

As we were talking, a myriad of reporters, cameras, and microphones descended upon us. Frederic worked methodically and gracefully despite the bright lights and big crowd. The whole scene began to feel like a press conference, with reporters throwing questions to Frederic and jotting notes on pads. It reminded me of a crowd in New York City that had unexpectedly crushed in on me and some model friends one day, but this was even more intense. Frederic had just published a book, and it was creating quite the frenzy.

He told the reporters he was enjoying working on my hair because it was naturally blond. I had not colored my hair at that point.

"I like things fresh and natural. She has a fabulous hair color."

I just smiled. *Thanks, Mom and Dad, for good genes.*

Eventually, the media frenzy died down. Frederic continued my haircut, and we had the chance to talk. We chatted about modeling, hair, his salon, and my own budding career. I'd only been working in the modeling industry for nine months, and I was plagued with concerns about my birthmark.

I pushed back my bangs, showed him my imperfection, and asked for his honest opinion. "You see a lot of beautiful and famous women. Do you think I should get this fixed? Will it make me more successful?"

God spoke through him that day. He said with his fabulous French accent, "Absolutely not. You are beautiful just like you are. You are a natural, and I barely notice that mark."

"Really? You didn't notice it?"

"No, I didn't. I would not touch it or get it fixed. Just be yourself. You are beautiful, and you are going to do just fine as a model."

I learned some valuable tips during that haircut, like how to create volume in my hair. "Back-combing or teasing your hair can be damaging," Frederic told me. "Let me show you a healthier, easier way to create volume." He took his fingers to my scalp under my hair and rubbed the crown with a circular motion. I tried it, too, and have used this trick on my hair ever since.

As we were talking, a producer walked over. "It's show time!"

We all made our way backstage, and Frederic stayed with the models and calmed our nerves. He had a warm, laid-back manner, and his friendliness put me at ease.

Quite soon, it was time for us to go onstage. "Frederic, ladies, you're on," the producer said. The curtain opened, and we made our entrance onto the runway. I stood on the left side of Frederic, and another model stood on his right. The three of us walked down the runway arm in arm, stopping when the emcee approached us. He interviewed Frederic about his new book and about the haircut and style he had given me just moments before.

Toward the end of the show, all the models took the stage together. The models Frederic had chosen were joined by thirty or so others, showcasing various designers. We all wore white dresses that had a portion of the flag on the dress and the train. Each model held the train of the model in front of her, and when we walked single file, we looked like a giant American flag blowing in the breeze. The designers had done a fabulous job creating that visual, timely piece of art, and I felt blessed and patriotic to be on the runway with such an ethnically diverse group of women. We were truly a reflection of America.

The encouragement and advice I received that night gave me the boost, inspiration, and confirmation I needed to navigate the ups and downs of the industry. I knew I was on the right path.

The following day, the models chosen by Team Fekkai worked at a hair show specifically arranged to help Frederic promote his new book as well as his salon and hair products.

About six months later, I received a call from my agent, Anne. "Do you want to work for Frederic Fekkai again at the Midwest Beauty Show?"

"Do I? Of course! I'm so glad he asked me back."

At the end of that show, I gave Frederic a small gift of thanks, to let him know how much I appreciated the encouragement and opportunities he had given me. Not only was I paid well, but he and his staff showed me great respect.

That was the last time I saw Frederic, as he only traveled for about a year to promote his book. He came alongside me while I was young and inexperienced, and he showed me I could accomplish significant things if I stayed true to myself, kept believing, and didn't give up. I felt like a little girl clunking on the keys of a piano, while a master pianist sits next to her, playing an amazing melody that incorporates her feeble attempts at a tune. I am thankful our paths crossed at such a pivotal time in my life and career.

Chapter 2

Trailblazer in the Making

*I want little girls to grow up knowing they can
do anything, even play football.*
JEN WELTER, THE NFL'S FIRST FEMALE COACH

My modeling adventure began in 1996 at a youth camp in
Missouri. I was there as a chaperone, seeking respite from my work at the
YMCA. But I was on my own spiritual quest that summer as well, and I was
about to learn that God had another reason for me to be at Camp Standlee.

Break was almost over, and I was looking forward to my senior year at
Christian Life College. Earlier that summer, I had begun seeking God's
direction for my future. I was anxious to figure out where I would work or
minister when I graduated from CLC. Plus, there was this guy who had
captured my attention. I was wondering if he was "the one."

In searching for my answers, I decided to fast. A one-day fast grew
into a three-day fast, and from there a forty-day liquid fast. If Jesus could
fast for forty days on just water, I thought I could surely fast for forty days

on just liquids. And so I had been living for weeks on soup broth, coffee, V8 juice, and Carnation Instant Breakfast shakes.

One night, I walked into the chapel with a lot of questions and very few answers. The worship band was warming up, and their gentle music drew me in. The energy of dozens of teenagers filled the air. I looked around for a seat.

Another youth leader, Mike, greeted me. "How's it going? I heard you're participating in the camp triathlon tomorrow. I bet you're going to win."

"Thanks for your vote of confidence, but I'm actually at the end of a long fast. I'm going to have to trust Him just for the strength to complete it."

Mike looked surprised. "Wow, are you sure you should take on this physical challenge right now?"

I told him I wasn't worried. I knew I could finish the fast and still swim, canoe, and run with the campers. Heck, I'd swum around an entire island the summer before with the University of Minnesota–Duluth triathlon team. This race paled in comparison. And a competition was brewing between Megan, one of the most athletic girls in our youth group, and me.

After our time of prayer and singing, the chapel speaker made his way to the platform. A hush fell over the crowd, and I leaned in to hear what he had to say.

"I know that God has uniquely called each one of you to fulfill a purpose He has specifically designed for you," the speaker said. "I want to call you forward in groups for prayer. For the first group, I want you to come forward if you feel like God is calling you to full-time ministry— perhaps to be a pastor or a missionary, maybe to work for a church in some capacity. For the second group, I want you to come forward if you feel called to the workplace, maybe as a doctor, a lawyer, a teacher, or a firefighter. And finally, for the last group, I want you to come forward if you feel like God is calling you to do something unique for Him. You may

32

not know exactly what it is yet, but you know He has a unique assignment that will use your gifts, and you haven't seen others do it. You are called to be a pioneer for Him and to blaze a trail for others."

Something sparked inside me. The speaker had just put words to thoughts that I had not verbalized to anyone. Filled with anticipation and relief, I walked forward and stood with the third group.

The speaker addressed us directly. "You will pave your own path with God," he said. "You are called to be pioneers, to be waymakers. He will lead you, and you will clear a path that others will follow. It won't be easy, but God will go with you. He will make a way for you."

As much as it scared me, I realized that being a Christian didn't mean I had to live a boring, conventional, or predictable life.

Bring it on, God. Let the adventure begin!

I knew God had something special for me to do. Would it be a triathlon career? I thrived on running, biking, and swimming, and I had worked my way up to be one of the top amateurs in my area. Could this be the unique way He was going to use me? Or did God have some other avenue for me to pursue as a pioneer?

I stepped outside into the warm summer air. As I walked back to my cabin, a renewed sense of hope filled my soul. I took a deep breath and exhaled. My concerns were gone, and a new sense of anticipation replaced the worries as I pondered how I would be a pioneer for Him.

The next morning before the triathlon, I had a long talk with Jared, Eric's best friend at college. After a lengthy conversation about my feelings for Eric, Jared got exasperated.

"For goodness sake," he said. "Why don't you just tell the guy how you feel? If you sense God directing you to share with him, quit talking to me and go talk to Eric."

"You're right, I need to face my fears and step out in faith. Thanks for the kick in the pants."

I turned my attention to the race. Although I felt spiritually and mentally strong, my physical strength wasn't there. I was sluggish in the Missouri heat, and the lack of nutrition zapped my energy. Nevertheless, I finished in second place and felt relieved as I downed a bottle of Gatorade.

I headed back to the cabin, contemplating what would happen when I got home. *At least I'm getting some answers here.*

Chapter 3

Unexpected Stranger

God can't steer parked cars.
FRED JOOB

Three years later, I hurried through the doors of the hotel so I wouldn't be late for the focus group I'd been paid to participate in that evening. It was 1999, and Eric and I were newlyweds. I worked full time as the manager of a local drop-in center for teens, but I was always looking for ways to make some extra cash to set up our first apartment together. So I signed up to participate in paid focus groups as often as possible.

In the lobby, I came to an abrupt halt and took in the sea of beautiful people surrounding me. Tall, lanky young men and gorgeous, svelte women milled about the room. *Are these people here for the focus group?*

Glamour floated around me like a soft cloud, and a certain energy—a mixture of excitement and nerves—filled the air. As I made my way down the hall, looking for my designated room, I glanced back at the young people. I felt drawn to them, and I wondered who they were and what they were doing in the hotel.

And then I saw the sign: *Model and Talent Search*. My curiosity was diverted, however, by a second sign that pointed me in the direction of my group.

I walked into the room and chose a seat next to some friendly looking women in the back. As we waited for further instruction on how things would play out that night, I kept thinking about the model search in the lobby.

Unexpectedly, the lady next to me turned and said, "I hope you don't think I'm strange for saying this, but you have a beautiful face. I think you should model. You should be out there instead of here." She gestured toward the front lobby.

My mouth dropped open. "This is amazing. I know we've never met before, but I've been praying with my husband that if I'm meant to pursue a career in acting or modeling, a stranger would tell me so. You are an answer to my prayers!" I felt like throwing my arms around her, but I resisted the urge.

"Well, I guess you have your answer then. I think you'll be a successful model, and I wish you all the best!"

I sat a little taller, and I could barely concentrate the rest of the evening. I still participated in the group, but focused, I was not.

I've often heard that the will of God is like a nagging voice inside your head that won't go away until you act on it. My mom had encouraged me for years to enter pageants and pursue a career in the business, but I hadn't personally pondered modeling until Sarah from church took a picture of me that won an award at her community college. I'd also received encouragement from strangers who approached me on the streets of Chicago, as well as the photographer at the YMCA where I'd worked during college.

Maybe it isn't just Mom trying to flatter me. Is this the kind of pioneer God wants me to be, a Christian model?

Modeling was Plan B for me. Until recently, I had been pursuing a career as a triathlete. But injuries from two separate accidents—one on a bike four years before and another in a car two years after that—had slammed the door shut on my dream to be a professional athlete.

I had been praying and discussing the possibility of modeling with Eric ever since. When I first told him I had this crazy idea, he said, "I totally think you have what it takes to do this. Besides, I always wanted to marry a model." So I had my husband's approval, and now God had given me the green light too.

Still, I had many questions. *Is this even a realistic possibility for my life? I'm twenty-seven years old already. Most models start much younger. Am I physically perfect enough for this business? Can I handle the temptations and challenges I'm likely to face? Will I have to compromise my values to make it?* I'd lived the party lifestyle before I became a Christian, and I didn't want to go down that path again. God and my marriage had to come first. Could that fit with a modeling career?

Despite these questions, I felt an underlying peace that God was leading me here. I had my answer. I was meant to pursue a career in modeling.

The only problem was that I didn't know a single person in the industry, and I didn't have the slightest clue how to get started. I was excited about the whole adventure, but where should I go from here?

Chapter 4

Fresh Start

He who is not courageous enough to take risks
will accomplish nothing in life.
Muhammad Ali

Not long after I attended that focus group, I was driving home from work when the idea hit me. *Go to the library, and you will find answers there.* I turned my car around right away.

To my chagrin, I found only one book on the topic of modeling. It was from the Wilhelmina Modeling Agency out of New York and had chapters about getting started, making composite cards, and finding an agent. It all seemed overwhelming. The book contained nothing specific about modeling agencies in Chicago, but I checked it out anyway.

I need to find someone to guide me through this. The internet was not well known or widely used in 1999, and Google did not exist to help me in my search. But not long after, I ran into Erica, my sister-in-law, at Eric's parents' house. "I know you're thinking about getting into modeling," she said. "I want to show you this."

She handed me a flyer for a talent search sponsored by Barbizon Modeling School. Barbizon's motto was " Train to be a model or just look like one." My understanding was that Barbizon was a program for preteens and teens like Erica, who attended a class with her peers once a week. She learned how to walk the runway, basic acting skills, and proper etiquette. The program was designed to teach self-care and confidence and prepare the best students for careers in modeling.

"I think you should go," she said. "I've seen adults at Barbizon, so you never know."

Two weeks after that conversation, I found myself walking into another hotel. I was struggling with my doubts. *What am I doing here? Am I really cut out for this?*

I smoothed my skirt and wiped my glistening palms as I made my way into the ballroom where the model search was being held. I found a seat in the middle of the room, and before long a middle-aged stepped to the podium to address the audience. She had short blond hair, and her makeup and nails were impeccable. She wore a fashionable black shawl, and I thought she looked very professional and polished as she spoke to the modeling hopefuls.

"I'm sure a number of you have questions about the modeling industry, and I want to address as many of them as possible. This is a business, and you can be as successful as you strive to be. But some people in this industry get involved in drugs and alcohol." She held up two fingers about an inch apart. "If you do that, your career will last about this long."

I was relieved. I didn't want to get caught up in that lifestyle again.

The woman went on. "People who succeed in modeling and acting see it as a business and take it very seriously." A sense of excitement and anticipation surged through me. *Now you're talking my language. I feel like I'm on the right track here.*

After the opening seminar, the attendees all lined up to speak to agents who were there. When my turn came, I approached the lady who had first addressed the group.

"How did you find out about our model search today?" she asked me.

I explained that my sister-in-law went to Barbizon, and that I wanted to pursue the industry but didn't know how to start. "I thought I could get some answers here."

"I agree, you have come to the right place. Let me ask, how old are you?"

"Well, I'm twenty-seven years old." When she found out how old I was, the woman nodded. "You're the perfect age to be in this business. You've taken care of yourself and look younger, so that will be a plus. But your maturity will benefit you and help you have a long-lasting career."

I hadn't expected to hear that. As she talked, she looked directly into my eyes. Her words washed over me like a refreshing rain. I needed encouragement and advice, and I sure was getting it! It was another confirmation that I was moving in the right direction.

"I don't think you should head to New York for your model quest," the woman said. "Everyone there will be much younger. I think you'll be better suited to get some training at Barbizon, and they can get you started right here in the Chicago market."

I took the speaker's advice and set up an appointment with Barbizon. They recommended that I sign up with a private teacher, who could accommodate my work schedule. I agreed, relieved I would not have to make a fool of myself in front of a group of people.

Still, I was nervous the first time I walked into the imposing high-rise in the heart of Chicago where the Barbizon school was located. Mrs. McMorrow, the director of Barbizon Chicago, greeted me. She was an elegant older woman with a sophisticated hairstyle and the lightest ice-blue eyes I'd ever seen. She was warm and kind as she led me to a small room equipped with an elevated runway. A woman wearing black, fitted clothes and high-heeled boots was waiting for me.

"This is Mrs. Newport," Mrs. McMorrow said, "and she will be your private instructor." I extended my hand and noticed that the teacher was at least ten years older than me, but she radiated youthful energy with her long blond hair and ruby lips.

I sure hope she can transform my tomboy ways over these next ten weeks! After growing up with four brothers and a slew of animals, I needed all the help I could get.

Mrs. Newport and I hit it off right away, but during our first few sessions I often felt like Julia Roberts's character in the movie *Pretty Woman.* I didn't have the first clue about proper etiquette, fine dining, how to walk up stairs, or how to get into a vehicle properly while wearing a skirt or dress. Mrs. Newport taught me all those things and more. We studied the color wheel so I could wear things that looked best on me to auditions and jobs. I learned how to carry myself, walk the runway, pose, and turn.

I often doubted I could be transformed and found the lessons difficult and perplexing, but my Finnish ancestors left me a lot of *sisu* (guts and determination), so I committed to the training. It helped that both Mrs. Newport and I kept a sense of humor throughout the process.

I walked into one of our final sessions and said, "I'm ready to get started! When can I get my pictures taken and composite cards done?" I grinned at her. "And do you want my autograph now or later?"

Mrs. Newport smiled back. "Soon, very soon. First, though, I want to prepare you for this business. Not everyone you meet will be friendly like you Minnesotans. I want to role play with you today and make sure you're ready."

We spent the afternoon practicing mock phone conversations. She would play a disgruntled client, barking orders and yelling at me. My job was to stay calm and speak kindly in return.

This lesson in always taking the high road was fabulous advice that I would use many times throughout my career. It helped me learn to handle the unkind critiques I would sometimes face as I went to various auditions and jobs. People complained about everything—from my hands that were too veiny and my knees that were too knobby to "the side of your forehead seems to have some shadow in these photographs. What is that?"

I was often told that I was too big for a job or too muscular. Other times I was told that I was too small or not curvy enough. I once auditioned to be a "fit model" for Harley Davidson. I had been in their catalog and even modeled their clothes at a dealer meeting in Milwaukee, but I was told I was not well endowed enough to be the live mannequin that the designers used while they made the clothes.

I told myself over and over, "Just be yourself, kill them with kindness, and take the high road."

In our ten weeks together, Mrs. Newport covered all the bases. I shed a lot of my tomboy ways and a few extra pounds, but I still had a lot left to learn when I graduated. It was just the beginning.

I was brimming with hope and eagerness to get started as I walked out of Barbizon that day, not realizing it would take me a year and a half to break into the business and start working steadily.

Chapter 5

Total Transformation

*Until you're ready to look foolish, you'll never
have the possibility of being great.*
CHER

On a lazy summer afternoon in 2000, I walked out of the Crowne Plaza Hotel in Elgin and into the warm sunlight. It was months since I'd graduated from Barbizon, and I was still trying to figure out how to really break into the modeling business.

A shuttle bus approached, and my heart pounded as I waited with a group of beautiful women to climb aboard. *What am I doing here?*

Just then, a white convertible pulled up behind the bus, and the smiling brunette behind the wheel waved at me. "Do you want to ride with me?"

She looked like she was up for an adventure. I hesitated only a moment before I accepted her offer.

Heck, I already jumped in the deep end when I registered for this pageant, so I might as well go all the way.

As I got into the car, I asked her, "Are we allowed to drive to the theater?"

"I think it's okay. There's not enough room for all of us on that bus," she said with a wave. "So tell me, where are you from?"

Lee and I talked the whole drive to the Hemmens Theater in Elgin, a suburb just north of Chicago. I told her how I'd heard about the Mrs. Illinois pageant through a friend at church. The friend had introduced me to a former pageant winner, who helped me register and coached me on what to expect.

At the pageant rehearsal, I'd met a number of the other contestants, including a tall, lanky redhead who clearly had experience and confidence. My coach told me she thought it was probably this woman's "year to win." I wondered how she could figure that out in advance, but I also noticed that the redhead had purchased several pages in the pageant program and there were many photos of her throughout the book. Contestants were allowed to purchase a page to promote themselves and the companies and individuals that sponsored them, but I'd thought it was limited to one page per contestant. I still had much to learn.

The Mrs. Illinois pageant was broken into four categories: interview, costume, swimsuit, and evening gown. We sat down for our interviews in the hotel, and I found out right before going into the room that my coach's husband was a judge. I swallowed hard. Had she already discussed me and the other contestants she'd coached with him? The news threw me off guard. I decided to follow Mrs. Newport's advice. *Take the high road, Amy. Just be yourself. Kill them with kindness. Trust God with the results.*

The interview went well despite the nerves I kept trying to stuff down. The man did acknowledge he was my coach's husband. I did my best to answer the questions but felt distracted with the recent revelation.

The following evening, we all took the stage for the competition. My stomach was in knots, but I exhaled deeply and mustered up every ounce of courage I had. Then I paraded out on stage in my one-piece bedazzled swimsuit and three-inch acrylic heels that reminded me of Cinderella's glass slippers. I hoped I looked half as elegant as she had the night of her ball.

Over the sound of my heart beating in my chest, I could hear at least fifteen of my family members and friends in the audience cheering for me and carrying me through this whole escapade.

Don't fall, don't fall. I made my way to the top of the stairs. I smiled with Vaseline-covered teeth and sucked in my stomach as I began my descent down the stairs that were positioned center stage. I could hear my coach in my mind: *Remember to smile, walk slow, don't look down. Keep your eyes out on the audience. Breathe.*

I was blinded by a spotlight as I approached the first stair, so on top of everything else, I was trying not to squint as I plastered on my smile. As I approached the second step, I made a quick decision. *Do I not look down and possibly slip and fall, or do I glance down and make it to the bottom standing?* I opted for the latter.

To make matters worse, as I was walking down the stairs as gracefully as possible, the emcee that evening gave the audience all my background information and statistics.

"And now we have Mrs. Rolling Meadows, Amy Joob. Amy has light blond hair, blue eyes, and weighs 145 pounds."

I heard several people in the audience gasp at that.

Oh my gosh, I shouldn't have given them my real weight. Some of the other girls were bigger than me, yet they all claimed to weigh 110 pounds. *Hey, these muscles weigh a lot. Don't judge me.* I pushed down the insecurities and kept smiling as I paraded around the stage. I smiled at the judges and prayed I could walk smoothly in my heels that seemed to be squeaking a bit with every step.

The whole experience reminded me of *Miss Congeniality*, the movie starring Sandra Bullock as an FBI agent who had to go undercover to play a beauty pageant contestant. Just like Sandra Bullock's character, I felt totally out of my element. I had been a successful triathlete; I'd focused all my attention on building strength and speed. Now here I was, trying to walk like a graceful doe across this stage.

As I stood and faced the scrutiny of the judges, another thought bothered me. A few weeks before, my coach had said, "You know that the pageant judges consider beauty of face as 25 percent of a contestant's overall score. You have that mark on your forehead, and I really think you should look into getting it fixed." She slid a business card across her desk. "This is my plastic surgeon's phone number. Give him a call. The consultation will be free."

Her comment had taken me totally off guard. I was very aware of my birthmark, but most people told me they had never noticed it or barely noticed it. No one had ever told me I should get it "fixed" before! I didn't call, but instead decided to trust God with results.

The incident blew back through my mind as I stepped onto the stage, but I'd also received some great advice from a woman named Jeri at church earlier that week. She told me she would be praying me through this pageant journey. "Picture yourself like Esther in the Old Testament," she said. "When you walk out on stage, hold your head high. Know that God is calling you to do this, and He is there with you. Imagine yourself walking into the King's presence." I focused my thoughts on that, and even when I was in the spotlight, it gave me great comfort and peace.

I didn't win the pageant that weekend. I didn't even make it as a finalist. Was it my birthmark or the fact that I looked down when I walked the stairs? Was I too muscular and more athletic than the other contestants? Or maybe because I didn't live in an affluent suburb like most of them? I'll never know.

To no one's surprise, the redhead my coach had pointed out as the favored contestant won the pageant. Eric met her husband backstage and learned it was her seventh time as a contestant. Pageants, then, were like almost everything else in life. You had to stay persistent and pay your dues.

I may not have won that pageant, but I did gain a boatload of confidence, a lifelong friend in Lee, and a half-page spread in the local newspaper. I hadn't won the pageant's costume contest, but I think the reporter from the *Daily Herald* thought I should have—they ran a great article and picture of me modeling my Cubs costume onstage.

Most importantly, I realized that when God calls you to do something, it might be challenging, but He will bring you the people you need. Eric, his dad, my supervisor at work, and even my supervisor's mom all helped me create that Cubs costume. And my family members and friends in the audience supported me too.

That was the only pageant I ever entered, but I would not trade that experience for anything. It taught me that there is joy in the journey and that having the support of your loved ones is priceless. And I had to draw on that experience not long after that weekend, as I was about to need all the courage I could muster to walk, talk, and carry myself with confidence, grace, and poise.

Chapter 6

Nailed It!

*Don't limit yourself. Many people limit themselves to what
they think they can do. You can go as far as your mind lets
you. What you believe, remember, you can achieve.*
MARY KAY ASH

I still didn't have a clear direction about what my next steps should
be to get into modeling. My new friends had given me contacts for a few
photographers, so I started there. Before I could approach agencies or
clients, I needed to get a composite card made. Comp cards featured a
model's headshot on the front and three or four different looks on the
back. Agencies wouldn't take me seriously without one, and once I found
representation, I'd be expected to give copies of the cards to clients as
part of the audition process.

I called Dan DuVerney, a photographer in Chicago. I liked Dan as
soon as I talked to him, but I had a problem. Photo shoots were expensive.

How would I get the money to pay for the necessary clothes, the photo shoot, and the cost of printing comp cards? *This might require a miracle!*

My parents had helped us pay for my modeling school tuition, but I couldn't ask them for something more.

At the time, Eric and I were helping some friends launch Northwest Family Church at a movie theater in the suburbs of Chicago, not far from our apartment. We volunteered and assisted the pastors every Sunday, and we all enjoyed living life and finding community together. A perk of hosting the church in a movie theater was that we got to see sneak previews of new releases—but the downside was that every Sunday we had to put together our sanctuary almost from scratch. Eric helped set up the onstage lighting, sound, and production, while I led the team that prayed over each of the theaters.

Eric and I had a close relationship with the pastors. Our goal was to do church in a new and unconventional way. We routinely met with the staff for breakfast at a local café called White Alps to brainstorm various ways we could reach unchurched people in the community.

As we were getting ready to go to breakfast one week, I heard that still small voice. *Ask Pastor Darrin for the money for the modeling shoot.* I can't say that I wanted to follow through. The very idea seemed counterintuitive. *Don't pastors need money? Aren't they the ones that ask you to give to the church?*

I talked it over with Eric. "What do you have to lose?" he asked. "If he says no, that's your answer. Or he might say yes, and you'll be glad you followed through."

The notion did not go away. In fact, the voice grew louder. *Ask Pastor Darrin; ask Pastor Darrin.* That week we met him for breakfast, and I summoned my courage as our meeting was wrapping up. With shaky hands holding a coffee cup, I blurted out, "Pastor Darrin, there's something I need to ask you."

"What is it, Amy?"

"I need money for my first photo shoot, and God put it on my heart to ask you. Would you be willing to help me pay for it?"

I half expected him to tell me I was crazy. Instead, he said, "Sure, we can help. How much do you need?"

"A thousand dollars?"

He didn't hesitate. "I can get a check to you later this week."

Wow.

"Thanks so much, Pastor Darrin. I've been praying about how to get the money. Eric and I didn't want to put it on a credit card. This is such a blessing."

Pastor Darrin and his wife, Amy, came through for me in a big way that week. They were the catalysts who helped me launch my modeling career. It was another confirmation that I was on the right path.

A few weeks later, I arrived at Dan DuVerney's brownstone studio on the west side of Chicago. I took in the vaulted ceilings, brick walls, and wooden floors. Upbeat music played in the background, and a dog came out to greet me. *What a sweet setup here.*

Dan welcomed me with a warm smile, and I immediately felt relaxed. "Come on in, make yourself comfortable. I'll show you where you can hang your things and change, and then I want to introduce you to my makeup artist, Trypheana."

By the makeup chair was one of the most beautiful African American women I have ever met. She looked like a model herself.

Trypheana studied my face. "I'm going to focus first on your eyebrows. Once we get a good shape there, they will totally frame the rest of your face."

I learned many tips from her that day about makeup, colors, false eyelashes, and more. She took her time, explained each step, and turned me into a work of art. To this day, Trypheana remains one of my favorite makeup artists.

She and Dan gave me a consultation as they worked. They told me which agencies were reputable in the business and which ones I should avoid. I left with a list of modeling agents as well as trade show agents.

When it was time to start taking pictures, Dan said, "It's time to relax and have some fun!" He cranked up the music and quickly had me laughing with his silly sense of humor. He created such a relaxed environment that all my fears melted away. We focused first on getting a great headshot, and then I put on the suit I wore in the Mrs. Illinois pageant interview and posed for a business look.

Eric came to the shoot later, and we took some "lifestyle" shots as a couple to show my versatility. The whole experience made me hungry to do more work in still photography as a print model. *I can really see myself doing this for a living.*

I'm glad that experience was so positive, because it made the waiting period that followed a little easier to handle. After I got my comp cards printed, I submitted them to various agencies in Chicago, around the Midwest, and even across the United States. I included a letter that stated, "I'm a professional model in Chicago, and I'm seeking representation from your agency. I have included a comp card and a résumé for your review. My contact information includes . . ."

On my résumé, I listed all the modeling jobs I had done as a teen in Minnesota. I wasn't paid for any of the work, but I gained experience from these jobs. I was grateful for the time I'd auditioned for and won a spot on the Miller Hill Mall fashion panel in Duluth. I didn't know then how important that experience would be, but it had led to a handful of still modeling jobs I did at Maurice's, a trendy mall store, runway shows at the mall, a Paul Mitchell hair show, and a bridal show for the historical society in Duluth.

I'd even done my very first print job for Nathan Bentley in Duluth for his then start-up screen printing business. That was in 1989, my junior year in high school, and I modeled with a set of Duluth-themed beach towels that featured the Aerial Lift Bridge.

Later I discovered I should have included a self-addressed stamped envelope with each package, and I should only focus on agencies in and around Chicago and Milwaukee. So six months after I sent out that first batch of letters, I sent out a second round. This time I got some positive feedback. I received not just one, but a few acceptance letters!

Models and actors seek agents because they are the best path to finding auditions and work. Agents also protect their models and ensure that we get paid. Sometimes a model will agree to be exclusively represented by a single agency. But some agencies aren't connected to enough jobs or auditions to keep their models busy. The people I'd met in the industry all recommended I sign up with several agencies and be multilisted. I was already listed with Royal Agency in Schaumburg, Illinois, but after I sent out the comp cards, I was accepted by Lori Lins in Milwaukee, Lily's, and Baker and Rowley in Chicago. I went to each agency in person to register and get started, and my career started to take shape. The dream was becoming a reality.

Chapter 7

Snowstorm Surprise

*I learned that courage was not the absence of fear, but
the triumph over it. The brave man is not he who does
not feel afraid, but he who conquers that fear.*
NELSON MANDELA

I drove cautiously into Chicago on a snowy, wintery day in
December of 2000. It seemed like a blizzard was brewing, but I'd left
home early so I could get to my audition on time. I had just left my job
managing the teen center and was really hoping to land this job.

My agent had told me that Sally's Beauty Supply was looking for
models, actors, and dancers to tour with them on their upcoming hair
show circuit. I wasn't trained as a dancer, but I thought I had a good
chance to be one of their models.

I parked on a snowy side street outside Joe Hall Dance Studio. I
prayed it would not snow so much that my car would be buried or that I
would get a ticket for blocking the snowplows. I snuggled into the collar

of my winter coat and tucked my model bag of supplies tightly under my arm. Then I opened the car door and braved the Chicago wind and snow. Inside, a group of hopeful-looking women were waiting to audition. Almost all the models were dressed in leotards, fitted clothing, and jazz shoes. *So here are the dancers I wonder where all the models are.*

I slipped into my high heels and followed them into the studio. We all sat down, and the choreographer, John, addressed us. "Ladies, thank you for coming out during a blizzard. I think this is a pretty decent-sized crowd, considering the snow. Sally's is looking for a team of twelve model/dancer/actors to go on a five-city tour starting in January. If you are here tonight, you will be auditioning for all three parts. We're looking for the total package."

I gulped, almost audibly. What had I gotten myself into? I thought the auditions were divided into categories, with models and dancers applying for different jobs. I hadn't had any dance training since high school cheerleading!

John was still talking. "So everyone, up on your feet. We're going to start with a couple of simple eight-counts. After we learn them as a group, I'm going to break you into groups of three or four, and then we will do some solo dances."

How did I get into this? I decided I might as well stay and give it my best shot, since I'd driven all the way into the city in the crazy weather.

"Girls, follow me. Five, six, seven, eight . . . step ball change, salsa to the left, salsa to the right, and now *pas de bourrée–*"

Pot of what? How do you do that?

I called on every ounce of experience I had as a figure skater, gymnast, cheerleader, and high school dance line dancer. With that and some *sisu*, I surprisingly kept up with most of the others. There were no more than twenty girls there, and Sally's wanted twelve.

I might have a shot at this thing.

On a break, I introduced myself to the woman closest to me. "Can I ask you for some help? Will you show me how to do that last eight-count John showed us?"

"Sure, I can help you out. Follow me. Five, six, seven, eight."

Thanks to Sherri's help, I worked out the kink and kept up with the others.

After we made it through the small-group competition, John told us, "I want to open this up to freestyle dance. I want you to move across the dance floor as if you were going down a long runway. Show me your best moves."

I watched one by one as these dancers moved gracefully down the floor. They leaped and twirled and looked completely stunning. I knew I didn't have those kinds of moves in my bag of tricks, but I had been a pretty good eighties-style hip-hop dancer. *I know what I'll do!*

When it was my turn, I prayed for some extra confidence to pull the moves off in my high heels, and then I turned around backward, gave everyone my open-mouth dance smile, and started to moonwalk across the studio. The girls laughed and clapped, and even John chuckled a bit. I may not have done a series of split leaps or *pas de bourrée*, but I got the crowd going!

In the end, the developing snowstorm worked in my favor. Only a fraction of the number of girls they had expected showed up. When John announced those who'd made it on the team, my name was on the list. I couldn't believe it!

I found out later that I was the only girl selected who was not a professionally trained dancer. I think my moonwalk, energy, and height won John over. He saw potential in me. God had answered my prayer for favor.

I choked back tears of joy until I could excuse myself and go to the bathroom.

After the break, those who made the team sat down to hear the details of the upcoming tour. The first thing John told us was, "Make sure you keep your appearance just as you look this evening. No drastic changes or haircuts. Keep your weight down. Everyone likes to overindulge this time of year, but you cannot gain weight over the holidays. You won't look right in your costumes, and you will not stay on this team."

I made a mental note to up my cardio and bring on the salad. *No Christmas cookies for me.*

I floated out of the dance studio that night, still in elated disbelief that I had landed my first big job. I couldn't wait to tell my agent, Anne.

The forty-mile drive home was treacherous, and I finally made it back to Lake Zurich with the worst migraine of my life. Eric welcomed me in, prayed for me, and took care of me that night. I loved that I could share my good news with him first. Eric had believed in me from the start. He'd encouraged me relentlessly to pursue my dream. The booking not only meant financial blessing, but further confirmation that I had made the right choice to step out in faith.

In January, I drove down to the dance studio again, grateful that there was no snowstorm this time. I was already nervous about whether I could learn the two or three dances we were slated to master before the tour started.

As soon as I arrived, though, John pulled me and two other girls aside. "We've decided that you three will be the "Face of Sally's" on this tour. You all have beautiful faces and perfect bone structure, and you will look amazing in the makeup they choose for you."

We all smiled, and he went on. "The good news is that you won't have to learn the dance routines. However, you'll still come to all the rehearsals and will get the same pay as the other girls. You will be doing theatrical runway between the numbers."

I'm sure John's decision had something to do with our face structures, but it was also about our level of dance experience. I felt nothing but relief as I watched how quickly these dancers picked up the moves. *Thank God I'm not trying to keep pace with them.*

Later in January, we all flew out to Long Beach, California. I roomed with Sherri, the dancer who had helped me at the audition. We got along well. I also got to know Kaja, our head model. She taught me a lot about the business side of modeling, including how to stand up for myself, act as my own agent, and negotiate fair rates. A lot of the advice she gave me stuck and has served me well over the years.

The hair show industry is a creative and artistic world. Stylists and cosmetologists attend shows to learn the latest styles, techniques, and trends. To maintain their credentials, they're also required to attend classes periodically, and hair shows are a good place for that training. Hair companies like Paul Mitchell, Big Sexy, Sebastian, and others use the shows to showcase their products, bringing in well-known stylists who can educate and entertain as they teach.

It's not surprising, then, that the "Faces of Sally's" painted on us were very avant-garde. It was a time-consuming process. We wore red catsuits with hoods up and black high heels. We each had a base of white makeup, and then the makeup artist added different colorful elements. Shannon had the prettiest face, as she had a butterfly over her eye. Lori's face was designed somewhere between Shannon's pretty face and the fierce look they gave me.

My makeup was the darkest look of the three, which was pretty ironic since I felt called to shine the love and light of God. Painted across my face were big black and red stripes. I realized I would need to develop some acting skills to fit this look. My normal personality is warm and outgoing, but for this role, I decided to project a mysterious circus clown. It was exciting to be disguised and portray another character, and my skills slowly developed over the course of the tour.

The tour took us to New York City, and the creative team decided to change up our look. This time, we wore black, skintight clothing with tall, black, high-heeled boots. Our faces stayed the same, but instead of hoods, the stylists put our hair up into hundreds of black bobby pins. It took nearly two hours to get all those pins in our hair, and the result was that we all had identical black, short pixie cuts. We looked punk rock and cutting edge, but the pins were heavy and painful after a while. I felt like I had a ten-pound weight wrapped around my head. I popped a couple of ibuprofen for the pain and enjoyed looking so dramatically different from my normal self. The crowd seemed to love it too.

While we were on a break between shows, the three of us were thirsty, and we decided to venture out into the Javits Center with our full makeup and costumes in search of water bottles. The convention center floor was filled with booths, stages, and people everywhere. It was hard to move through the crowd, and people stopped us repeatedly.

"Excuse me, ladies, can we get a picture with you?" Group after group asked us to pose, and we began to feel smothered.

All of a sudden, Lori shouted, "Girls, let's run!" The three of us made eye contact, smiled, and took off. The Face of Sally's became a black ocean wave, rolling through the crowd without stopping.

"What just happened?" I gasped as we found refuge behind some curtains.

"I know!" Lori said. "It's like they all thought we were famous. That was crazy!" We all laughed and caught our breath before we snuck back to our holding area, where we found water bottles waiting for us.

The Sally's dancers and models had a lot of downtime during the tour. We sat in hair and makeup and between the shows for hours each day. Show business is truly a hurry-up-and-wait experience. I took advantage of our break times to share my faith in Jesus with my new friends. I was able to talk at greater length with my fellow Face of Sally's models, and I had some really great conversations with Lori. She was ten years younger than me, a rhythmic gymnast who had been an alternate on the US Olympic team. She talked to me about her boyfriend and how she was trying to figure out the future of their relationship.

Also light blond, Lori could pass for my younger sister, but she was far more experienced as a model and dancer. She'd started when she was thirteen years old. Now, seven years later, she told me she was burned out and ready to focus on college. *And here I am at twenty-nine years old and just starting my professional career.*

Most people I shared my faith with were receptive, but one of the dancers got angry. "Not everyone wants to hear your stories about God. You should keep them to yourself."

I smiled and answered, "I'm sorry, I didn't mean to offend you. I will respect your space."

No matter how people reacted, I knew God had called me into this industry not just to make money or pursue a career but to let others know about His love. He made it clear to me from that very first job that I was a pioneer in this industry, and that I would have many opportunities to go undercover for Him. I may not have been an FBI agent like I first planned when I studied criminal justice at Auburn University, but I was doing some adventurous, meaningful work nonetheless.

Chapter 8
Mission Possible

*We're here for a reason. I believe a bit of the reason is to throw
little torches out to lead people through the dark.*
WHOOPI GOLDBERG

During the time I was traveling with Sally's, I had two profound
dreams that helped shape my perspective for years to come.

Eric had enrolled in Harper Community College, not far from our
home. He later transferred to DePaul University in Chicago, where he
earned his bachelor's degree in international business and marketing.
I worked part time at a local YMCA and started a cleaning business to
supplement our income between modeling jobs. I was registered with
a few agencies, but the work was still slow to trickle in. I hadn't quite
yet figured out that modeling is a constant hustle. When you're an
independent contractor, you're continually looking for the next job.
It can be exhausting, and I understood why so many models looked for
longer contracts and steady gigs.

Eric and I had just returned from a pilgrimage to Israel, where we saw soldiers walking the streets dressed in full uniform and carrying machine guns. At tourist sites like the Yad Vashem memorial, there were hundreds of firearms leaning against the outside of the building. We were told that everyone had to leave them outside of the buildings to show respect. Later, Palestinian leader Yasser Arafat's entourage passed our tour bus, and I saw men in black, shiny vehicles, wearing keffiyeh and dark sunglasses.

One night not long after we got back home, I fell asleep and found myself in a long, dark, underground tunnel, being chased by fierce soldiers who looked like terrorists. I looked for a way to escape, searching desperately for the proverbial light at the end of the tunnel. Then I looked up and saw a window, no, a door ahead. I ran toward what I hoped would be freedom. It seemed like the only way to avoid being captured.

I looked back over my shoulder, and the enemy soldiers seemed to be gaining on me. Suddenly, I heard my high school track coach in my mind, "Never look back in a race. Keep your focus straight ahead. It takes too much energy to look back—it could cost you the race!" This advice is affirmed in Philippians 3:13 (NET): "Brothers and sisters, I do not consider myself to have attained this. Instead I am single-minded: forgetting the things that are behind and reaching out for the things that are ahead."

The thought was an important element of my dream and a valuable principle I would carry forward into life—quit looking back at yesterday and instead move forward and focus on what God has for you today and in your future.

In my dream, I fixed my gaze straight ahead, and as I neared the door, light streamed through it. I burst through and felt hope and relief flood over me. I was completely enveloped in love and peace, and I smiled from ear to ear as I spun in circles in this amazing, lush, green promised land.

This is heaven. The beaming sunlight, the overwhelming sense of love, the complete sense of safety—fulfillment and contentment oozed into every fiber of my being. It was the most euphoric state I have ever experienced.

I knew that God in all His goodness was there, and I did not want to leave that place. I wanted to stay forever. But I basked in the rays of that light for only a short while before I heard His still, small voice. *"I have shown you the way out. Now go back and get the others. They need you to guide them to this place."*

I didn't want to go back in there. It was dangerous and life-threatening. Yet even as I thought that, I pictured those I loved and those He'd called me to reach. Specifically, I saw my family, friends, and those in the modeling industry. I knew I had to go back. I figured if He'd called me to do it, He would not only equip me but protect me as well.

I headed back into the tunnel, and soon enough, I found people running toward me—men, women, and children of various nationalities and ethnicities. I felt a sense of urgency and responsibility like none other. I didn't want to lose one person on my watch. The protective side of my personality that drove me to get a degree in criminal justice met the part of me that cares for the souls of others with my second degree in pastoral studies.

We could hear the enemy behind us, and we kept pressing forward. As I came alongside the people in that tunnel, I became their cheerleader, guide, motivator, and advocate. I kept them rallied and moving forward. I made sure the smallest and slowest person did not get left behind as we kept moving fast enough to get away. Occasionally, people would stop at a window or door and try to get out, but I told them those were not the right ways. I kept urging them on toward the end of the tunnel. I even started to relax in my position; I enjoyed the physical challenge of running and overcoming obstacles on our way to the final destination.

We eventually made our way to the end, and I flung open the door to the vast promised land. I held it open as person after person went flying through that door into peace and freedom, and then I woke up.

The dream, I decided, symbolized my Christian faith and what I felt God calling me to do. I was once completely lost, and God came to save me through His Son, Jesus Christ. Jesus showed me the way out of darkness, addiction, and pain. After I gave my life to Him, He told me to go back and help the others.

And so when I woke up, I had fresh motivation, desire, and urgency to complete that mission. I had the reassurance that I would be able to handle whatever came my way. And in the years that followed, God came through for me in big ways. Whenever I got overly concerned about my appearance, the work, the pay, or some other aspect of the modeling industry, I could hear Him reassuring me. *Amy, this is not about you. This is about Me. I have called you to be here, and I will keep you here. Keep helping and sharing My love with others. I will make a way for you.*

Not long after that first dream, I had a second one that answered more questions for me. I had been struggling with my perspective on success and money. I'd also been questioning which kinds of jobs I should take and which ones I should turn down. *Am I too ambitious? Should I even be ambitious as a Christian?*

One night, I dreamed that two tall, impeccably dressed businessmen approached me. They wore dress pants, button-down shirts, and ties, and each carried a trench coat folded neatly over his arm. Each man handed me cash. I looked down at the bills, and written on them was "Trust your instincts and follow your ambitions."

Our exchange was very businesslike and official, yet the whole dream had an overriding tone of love. After the men left, I realized they must have been angels. God sent them to tell me that I could trust my instincts and that I was on the right path.

As I reflected on those dreams and the current path I was on, I realized most of my passions and life experiences were merging together. Eric and I loved Jennifer Garner's TV show, *Alias.* Jennifer's character, Sydney Bristow, was a double agent for the CIA, and she routinely went undercover. In the show, Sydney would costume herself in different outfits to fit in, but her real purpose was always the mission her agency sent her on.

Similarly, even though I was working as a model, playing characters, and going on various assignments, my real mission was being a Christian, shining my light, and looking for others I could reach for Him.

As I worked in the industry with this newfound perspective, I felt like I had found my sweet spot. I wore costumes and beautiful clothing and went to unique places, and sometimes people didn't understand what I was doing. I'd had to let go of my people-pleasing habits when I became a model, because a couple of Christian friends actively disapproved of my career choice. They wrote to me and told me I was making a big mistake. They warned me not to go into modeling or acting, because it might ruin my life and marriage. I might fall away from God completely.

What they didn't understand was that my underlying purpose in entering the industry was to be Christ's ambassador. I felt honored that God chose me and entrusted me with this position. It really took the pressure off as I learned to lean more on Him, to trust Him for favor and open doors. I often turned to 1 John 4:4 for reassurance. "He who is in you is greater than he who is in the world."

I came to accept that I would often be misunderstood. In the modeling world, I was known as the "good girl," the conservative Christian. In Christian circles, some people said I was too liberal and doing things that were borderline unbiblical.

Eric came home from his Bible study group one day and told me one of the guys in his group asked how he could let me go on modeling jobs and travel around the country. Eric's response was, "I think it's awesome that my wife is a model. I know she's doing exactly what God called her to do."

My husband always stood beside me, and I often received counsel from his dad, my father-in-law, as well. He and I talked once about which modeling jobs were acceptable to take. He said, "Keep God, keep Eric, and keep your clothes on. The rest of the jobs you do should be okay."

Eric knows I'm an open book with a soft conscience, and that made my calling easier on our marriage. I told him the good, the bad, the wonderful, the ugly, and everything in between about me and the people I interacted with daily. That built trust between us and kept our communication lines open when we were apart.

I felt fulfilled as a model, and God brought me numerous opportunities to share my faith, pray with others, and encourage people. And He brought many people along my path to guide, support, and encourage me as well. As my career gained momentum, I realized that the calling I felt at that camp all those years ago had come to pass. I had become a pioneer, and together with God, I was blazing a trail in the modeling world. When I stepped into uncharted territory, He met me there every time. And with each step of faith, He honored me with new opportunities.

Chapter 9

Trauma on a Tuesday

I always did something I was a little not ready to do. I think that's how you grow. When there's that moment of "Wow, I'm not really sure I can do this," and you push through these moments, that's when you have a breakthrough.
MARISSA MAYER

Breaking into the modeling industry was a feat in itself, and those early jobs felt like being on a crazy roller coaster. In 2001, I met another model and actor named Renee while working on the set of the television show, *What About Joan*. We hit it off, not only becoming friends but eventually prayer partners as well. Renee introduced me to an agency in California, and through them I booked my first trade show job, working for a company exhibiting their products at the Print '01 Convention.

Summer was turning into fall when I arrived at McCormick Place on the south side of Chicago. The convention center itself was completely overwhelming. I pulled up to a back lot and parked, not realizing I was in a lot used primarily by union workers. I began my trek through a long tunnel in search of the main entrance. I must have looked out of place in my bright red, vintage flight attendant ensemble because a man in a golf cart pulled up. "Hey, do you want a ride? It's a pretty long walk to the entrance." I hesitated but felt a peace about his invitation, so I hopped into the cart. The man dropped me off in front of the convention center's main doors and gave me directions to the south hall where I was working that day.

People were hustling and bustling up and down escalators everywhere. I recited his directions in my mind: *Up two flights of escalators, take a left, and walk until you see a large hall on the left.*

I could almost hear my heart beating, I felt so nervous. But as I rode the first escalator, a sign caught my attention. "Got convention tension? Relax." I focused on that word. *Relax.* God was sending me a timely message. I felt reassured in knowing that where He guides, He provides. I could trust Him to give me the grace and wisdom to handle this job.

The work that day was easier than I expected. I was one of seventy-five hostesses working for Heidelberg Printing Press. We helped facilitate the booth, greeted people, scanned badges, and oversaw the various departments within their enormous display. There was a lot to learn, and it was a lot of walking in high heels, but I told myself the paycheck would be worth it. Besides, Renee was there, so I had an ally.

On the third day of the convention, a Tuesday, I decided to take the train into the city to avoid the traffic. I'd never ridden the Metra commuter train alone before, but most of the ride went smoothly. I looked out the window as we whizzed by all the traffic on the expressway. *Thank God I'm not sitting there, stuck in that mess!*

We were nearing the Chicago station when cell phone after cell phone started ringing. *Is this normal? When the train arrives at the station, does everyone get phone calls?* My phone wasn't ringing. I watched the people around me, and they all seemed concerned. *Something doesn't feel right.*

I was too shy to ask a stranger what was going on, so I exited the train station and hopped into the nearest taxi for my first Chicago cab ride. "I need to go to McCormick Place, please." Even as I spoke to the driver, I noticed he had his car radio turned up.

"Do you know what is going on right now?" I asked.

I had a hard time understanding the driver's thick accent as he replied, "The World Trade Center in New York has been hit by a plane."

It was September 11, 2001.

As the driver pulled into the busy morning traffic, I thought about the time just a few years earlier when I had stood on the World Trade Center observation deck with my dad. The views of New York City were incredible.

I was still trying to wrap my head around the news as I jumped out of the cab and made my way into McCormick Place. I had to be at my station in the Heidelberg booth by nine o'clock, and I thrived on timeliness, but I also wanted to find out what was going on in New York.

Once again, my heart pounded as I made my way up the escalators, but this time for a different reason. A sea of people huddled around a television monitor in the main hallway, and I joined them. None of us spoke. A feeling of heaviness permeated the air.

I had experienced this feeling once before, on a smaller scale, when I was an intern for the Lee County Sheriff's Department in Alabama. One night we responded to a car accident where some college students had died at the scene. I will always remember seeing their lifeless bodies, still buckled into their seatbelts, in their overturned SUV.

Now I stood in a group of strangers as we watched the live coverage of the second airplane crashing into a tower. Black smoke and flames billowed out of the side of the building. I walked away before the towers fell, making my way slowly to the Heidelberg booth and the registration desk where I was assigned to work that day.

People in the trade show were all milling about. There was a sense of controlled chaos there. Some hostesses were at their posts, others were walking around in shock, and others were crying and trying to comfort one another. No one was hysterical, but we were all affected. Waves of words floated over me, and I suddenly realized they were calling it a terrorist attack.

What cities might be hit next?

It was a heart-wrenching, heavy day, and it wasn't even nine thirty in the morning yet.

I tried to call Eric but couldn't get through. The lines were all jammed. I whispered prayers, specifically invoking Psalm 91 and Isaiah 54:17 over Eric, myself, and everyone at McCormick Place.

God, please hide us all in the shadow of Your wing. I pray that no weapon formed against us shall prosper. Every tongue that rises up in judgment against us, I pray that You will condemn. Please protect us all here, and let every plan and attack of the Enemy be foiled in Jesus's name. Lord, please protect our families and our entire country, and let this all come to a quick end.

As I stood there, silently praying, a man walked up to the registration booth. He acted like nothing unusual was happening. "Excuse me, I have an appointment with so-and-so. Is he here yet?"

I had to tell him, "I'm sorry, sir, but I'm not sure. In light of everything that's happening in New York right now, I'm not even sure if the show is open today." He gave me a half-smile and walked away without asking any further questions.

I went to find Renee so I could process the situation with her. "Are you going to stay or go home?"

"I think I'm going to wait it out here," she said. "Otherwise, I'll just be sitting there alone, thinking about everything by myself. It might be better to stay here and finish out our job today."

Her words made sense. "Yeah. Okay. I'm going to stay too." Going back out and taking the train again made me more nervous than staying where I was.

Not long after, the president of Heidelberg Printing Press addressed our trade show staff. After he expressed his condolences about the events in New York, he basically said the show must go on. Print '01 would remain open for business. It was left to the discretion of the individual exhibitors and companies whether to close or stay open. Since Heidelberg had brought a lot of key staff from Germany and other parts of the world, and since airports were all closed and flights canceled for the foreseeable future, they would continue to work.

I was assigned a new hostess position at the booth's travel office, where several Heidelberg staff coordinated travel plans for their employees. But with all airports shut down and every plane grounded, my job title could have been called "grief counselor." A number of international employees waited in an anguished-looking line, hoping to book flights home as soon as possible. I couldn't imagine what it must feel like to be in a foreign country, thousands of miles from family and friends, in the midst of an attack like this. Some of these people were in the United States for the first time and had planned to visit New York City as soon as the trade show was over. Not anymore. It made me sad and mad at the same time.

I just need to focus and do my job. Right then, my job was to comfort, console, and counsel. We couldn't get anyone booked on flights home, so we just had to pass the time and try to keep everyone calm. It was a good life lesson for me: When I'm hurting, I can get my mind off my own troubles if I help others. If I focus on being positive and meeting the needs of others, somehow God ends up fixing me too. I once heard a pastor say, "If you take care of what's on the heart of God, He will take care of what's on your heart."

I found great solace as I left the convention center at five o'clock. The ride home was eerie. Barely anyone was on the roads, even though it was rush hour. The train station looked like a ghost town. Apparently, most people had evacuated the city earlier in the day as rumors spread that Chicago may be the next target.

I found my train, and the conductor on the platform said in a subdued voice, "The ride's free today. No charge." Only a few people sat, scattered and silent, throughout the cars.

As the train pushed northwest, taking me closer to home, I held back my tears. I wanted to cry for every person on that train, for the conductor, for myself and my family, for every person who had lost his or her life that day, and for all the family members who had lost loved ones. I wanted to cry for America and for our future. It would be a long time before I felt safe again, and even longer before things felt anything like normal.

I leaned heavily on God and His promises that day and in the days that followed. The tragedy reinforced my need to be near Him and trust Him for protection and blessing. I found comfort in the Scriptures; through journaling my thoughts, feelings, and fears; and from knowing that He is ultimately in control.

During that season, I often prayed Psalm 32:7–8 (NIV): "You are my hiding place; you will protect me from trouble and surround me with songs of deliverance. I will instruct you and teach you in the way you should go; I will counsel you and watch over you."

Chapter 10

Door to India

My philosophy is that not only are you responsible
for your life but doing the best at this moment puts
you in the best place for the next moment.
OPRAH WINFREY

A week later, I made my way again through the streets of busy downtown Chicago. The buildings loomed large above me. It was a rainy day, and traffic was heavy and intense. Driving through congested traffic was nerve-racking for me, and sometimes I didn't know which was worse— driving through the city trying to find yet another new building or going to the audition or job itself.

I strained my neck to read numbers as I made my way slowly down the street. Horns kept honking, and I tried to ignore them as I searched for the office building where I was supposed to meet Simi for coffee. Of course, once I finally located the right place, there was no street parking. I had to go to the nearest garage and pay to park.

Finally, I made my way into the high-rise and sat at a cozy table in the café. I watched office workers scurry in and out of the revolving doors. Despite the rain and traffic, the magic of big city life was beginning to win me over. I had grown up secluded in the woods; the fast pace, cultural diversity, and excitement here were intriguing.

Simi made her way over to the table, and we exchanged pleasantries. She owned a company called Strut Productions. A mutual friend from Barbizon had connected us, and we'd talked on the phone a few times. We seemed to share a kindred spirit from the start. She leaned in toward me as we sipped our cappuccinos.

"I believe we can help make each other successful. The way my husband, Nav, and I see it, and the way my friends see it, is that we can all help pull each other up. If one is raised up a level, they reach down and pull up the ones beneath them. And then when they are raised up, they reach down and pull up the others. Then we all reach the top and have one big party!"

That was a cool analogy. "I agree. Not only striving for your own success but helping others succeed too."

Simi and I developed a close friendship. She opened the doors for me to some amazing modeling jobs, like the fashion shows she produced at the House of Blues, the Daley Center, and Park West. We also did a number of East Indian bridal shows together. Each show had a fashion showcase, where models like me would walk the runway and showcase the designers' newest clothing lines. We modeled Indian clothing or bridal gowns sometimes, and other times we wore the latest trends from local designers. Simi's productions and our photos made it into *Sahara Magazine* on a number of occasions.

In the fall of 2001, Simi and Strut Productions partnered with the 20/30 Club of Chicago, an organization of young professionals, to do a benefit at Union Station for the Mercy Home of Chicago. Simi hired me to model, and I got to take Eric with me. We'd booked a room in a nearby hotel to make a weekend getaway out of it. He hung out with Nav and friends as I worked the show.

I wanted to pinch myself as I prepared that night. This was my first big fashion show, and my eyes grew like saucers when I took in the huge runway that extended halfway across the station's ornate Great Hall. In the dressing room, Simi pointed out my assigned clothing for the evening and the order of my outfits. I got settled in and laid out all my shoes, and we headed out to the runway for rehearsal.

The incident at the Twin Towers was still fresh in all our minds, and Simi and the event organizers didn't know if it was too early to bring a festive atmosphere to the party. However, we were doing a benefit for a good cause, and we took time to honor those who were lost before we started the evening rehearsal and activities.

As we prepared to start, I stepped back and soaked in the atmosphere of the majestic space, with its vaulted ceiling, chandeliers, stone, and tile. The room sparkled in the soft glow of candles. Waitstaff walked around with hors d'oeuvres, and men in black suits and ties mingled with pretty ladies in beautiful, sparkly cocktail dresses. Ice sculptures graced every corner; bars and food stations were arranged strategically throughout the hall.

As I took the stage for my first run, I was blinded by the spotlight and yet energized by the atmosphere. I started my strut down the long runway, moving my hips to the beat of the music. I relaxed as I went, confident that I looked absolutely stunning. The energy in the room was electric, and I made quick changes from outfit to outfit in the dressing room between my turns on the runway. The challenge of seeing how quickly I could change reminded me of my quick transitions in triathlons and added to the excitement of modeling each new ensemble.

As I modeled more often through Strut Productions, Simi and I grew closer, and we began to hang out with our husbands too. Eric and Nav joined a basketball league together and formed a team at Windy City Fieldhouse.

Simi and I would join the other wives every week to watch our husbands play.

We all hung out at Simi and Nav's place in Greektown after the games. Their apartment, in a west-side neighborhood near the University of Illinois at Chicago, was stunning with vaulted ceilings and big windows looking out on the Chicago skyline. Eric and I loved the location and happily dog-sat when Nav and Simi went out of town for the weekend. We would fall asleep under the twinkling lights and glow of the Sears Tower, just blocks away. It certainly was a contrast from the crickets and croaking frogs I had grown up with in northern Minnesota.

Simi and Nav were trying to conceive a baby during that time, and she and I had long talks in that apartment. I shared with her about my upbringing in Minnesota and my faith as a Christian, and she told me about her upbringing in Chicago and her religion as a Hindu. I prayed for her often. It wasn't long before Simi made the transition from dog mom to the mom of two beautiful children. She and Nav moved to a house out in the suburbs, and my days of modeling for Strut Productions slowed. The years we did work together left an indelible impression on me, though, and were happy stepping stones in my career.

Chapter 11

First Time in the Ring

You are someone else's miracle! God is setting up
divine appointments, and it is your job to keep them.
MARK BATTERSON

My thirtieth birthday was just around the corner, and I found myself doing some serious soul searching. Eric and I lived in a beautiful apartment in Lake Zurich, but my work was coming slowly, and even after I did a job it took thirty to ninety days to receive payment. Meanwhile, Eric was going to college.

Money was tight, to put it mildly. We really couldn't afford to pay our rent and living expenses along with college. We prayed together for direction, and God put Eric's parents on our hearts. We talked it over together.

"Is it possible to move into their basement? Is this a step backward for us?" I asked.

Eric, as always, was more pragmatic. "Maybe God is trying to make it easier for us to get on this new path. Even if it doesn't totally make sense, He can see the future."

"Yeah, it seems a little crazy, but I feel a peace about it. It may mean sacrificing some things."

"But in the end, it'll be worth it."

And so, the weekend of my thirtieth birthday, we moved into his parent's home. We ended up living there for three years, and during that time, God continued to bring provision and favor so we could move forward and fulfill what He called us to do. It was the stimulus we needed to propel us forward and get us established in the new careers He had for us both.

* * *

One cold, winter night a short time later, I drove out to Rockford, Illinois, to work at a live event for the World Wrestling Federation (WWF). At that time, professional wrestling was very popular, followed by loyal fans at events as well as on television. We would be filming an episode for the wrestling television program *The Heat on MTV*. My agent told me I would be one of three models playing The Godfather's escort. The Godfather was a main WWF wrestler; he once headlined *Saturday Night's Main Event* against Bret Hart for the WWF Championship.

My agent also told me I needed to take my own wardrobe and do my own hair and makeup, which was a relief. Often models are given specific clothes or costumes, and I had been worried that WWF would expect me to be in a bikini as the "ring girl" (which I had been asked to do a few times before at other events and had always declined). Using my own wardrobe would allow me to control a lot of the variables surrounding my image, and so as I drove to the venue, I felt a peace about the job.

I walked into the Rockford MetroCentre and was immediately surrounded by muscular men and women milling about behind the scenes. An air of professionalism and intensity emanated from these workers. They made me think of Muir Woods in Northern California. Wrestlers looked like huge, majestic redwood pines, shooting up to the sky all around me. Even in my highest-heeled boots and at six feet tall, I felt like a short, little evergreen tree compared to them. I felt comfortable, like I was back in Minnesota where my brothers and many other Scandinavians towered over me as well.

My contact person for the evening directed me to the holding area where the models and actors scheduled to perform that evening were gathering. "Wait here until we're ready to rehearse," she told me. "Make yourself at home. Eat and drink whatever you like."

I smiled and introduced myself to the other talent in the room. They all seemed a little nervous, just like me. I didn't want to eat, because I didn't want to look bloated on television, and I never drank alcohol on jobs. I wanted to make sure I could always think clearly, act professionally, and maintain my integrity. For me, drinking and work did not mix well, and I noticed that many of the younger models followed my lead. That night as we sat around and chatted, I prayed for doors to open so I could share my faith.

When it was time for rehearsal, we made our way into the arena. Wrestlers already in the ring were shouting at each other. I quickly learned that they were rehearsing too. Everything in a professional wrestling match is scripted, and the wrestlers on the circuit take their jobs as actors very seriously. They work out frequently, eat clean, and see the job as a professional business.

After our rehearsal, one of the younger models mentioned, "I really want to go over there and meet Hulk Hogan." The famous wrestler was standing a short distance away from us.

"I'll go over and meet him with you," I told her. We sauntered over and introduced ourselves. I was happy to find that he was approachable and friendly, not at all like his character in the ring. He answered questions and gave us autographs. I was impressed at how kind, hardworking, fit, and professional they all were.

We made our way over to The Godfather and had time to chat with him before our taping started. I could hear the roar of the crowd from backstage, where we were surrounded by sound and lighting boards, computers, headsets, and technology galore.

Watching WWF on TV made it seem like an out-of-control environment with egotistical athletes, but watching it from behind the scenes showed me that in reality, professional wrestling was a well-planned, choreographed, and smooth operation.

As we made small talk, I asked The Godfather, "So how did you get started in this business?"

He smiled. "Before I came on tour with the WWF, I was living crazy. One of these guys gave me a chance, and they helped me clean up my act. Now I'm eating well, working out, and staying away from crazy parties. I'm a lot healthier. So for me, the circuit isn't just a job; it gives me purpose."

"That is really awesome," I told him and started to share my own story about my past wild lifestyle. I just started to tell him about how I became a Christian when we were called for our turn in the ring.

It was almost eleven o'clock at night when I said goodbye to everyone affiliated with the WWF. Everyone was exhausted after the long day, and as the models stepped outside, we were wrapped up in darkness. One younger model mentioned that she'd parked a distance away from the Centre. I didn't want her to walk that far in the dark all alone. "Can I give you a ride to your car?"

She smiled at me and looked relieved. "That would be great," she said.

I wondered if God had put me there that night to look out for her. It seemed like divine appointments were materializing more often, which made my work more exciting and definitely more fulfilling.

Chapter 12

Mercy Moment

*This is what the LORD ... says: I have heard your
prayer and seen your tears. I will heal you.*
2 KINGS 20:5 NLT

Early in 2002, my mom called. "Have you heard about Jeff's wife?"

I hadn't talked to my cousin in a while. "No, what's going on?"

"I have some sad news. Kristen passed away suddenly, and Jeff is going through a hard time. I know you've reached out to him before. Maybe you can do that again?"

My heart hurt for my cousin, who was the same age as my oldest brother. "I've been doing more modeling work in Milwaukee. In fact, I have a job coming up with Harley Davidson soon. I'll try to see him then."

"That would be wonderful." Mom sounded relieved. "I think he could use all the encouragement he can get."

Jeff had been a Milwaukee police officer for years. He'd even been shot while off duty trying to stop a robbery, and I had gone to visit him in the hospital then. Miraculously, he'd recovered from his injuries, but I couldn't imagine recovering from this. To lose a spouse at a young age would be devastating.

Harley Davidson held a dealer meeting, an annual event at their Milwaukee headquarters. Their dealers came from around the country to check out the motorcycles, gear, clothing, and everything else that pertained to bikes and the industry. I was already booked for the event as an informal model, which meant I would showcase the latest Harley Davidson apparel by wearing it while walking around the meeting.

I called Jeff to tell him about my upcoming trip, and he welcomed my visit and even offered for me to stay with him. I agreed, glad to avoid the commute back and forth to Illinois.

After I finished my job the first day, I went to Jeff's townhouse. He wasn't working that night, and as he welcomed me in, I could see the heaviness and sadness on his face. "I'm so sorry to hear what happened," I said.

"Thanks for coming, Amy. I appreciate you being here."

I put my things down, and we sat at the table. Jeff told me about the accident and everything that happened. His pain and grief were palpable. After he finished his story, we prayed together. He said he was thinking about going to church again, and I encouraged him to find a small group or a support group as well. God could take the hardest things and turn them around in ways we couldn't imagine. Isaiah 61:3 (NIV) says that He will "bestow on them a crown of beauty instead of ashes, the oil of joy instead of mourning, and a garment of praise instead of a spirit of despair."

The next few days flew by, and when I left, I told Jeff, "Call me any time. I'm here if you need to talk or if you want to hang out. I'm coming up here more often for jobs and auditions." It was true. I'd just done a print job in the *Milwaukee Journal.*

Jeff smiled. "That would be good. I can take you to some of my favorite restaurants, or we could go to a Brewers game. Have you and Eric ever been to German Fest here?"

"No, but that sounds fun!"

As I drove home, I couldn't stop thinking about Jeff and praying for him. It was a burden I couldn't imagine having to carry. I prayed he would find a good church and loving people who would surround him and walk with him on the path of healing.

Chapter 13

Risky Business

Perseverance is failing nineteen times and succeeding the twentieth.
JULIE ANDREWS

It was a windy, blustery March day in Chicago. The modeling industry had taken an economic hit after 9/11, and I'd heard from several experienced models that the work wasn't as plentiful as it had been. Since my career had just been ramping up in the fall of 2001, I didn't know anything different, and maybe that was a good thing. Money was tight, but that meant I was trusting God to open the right doors as I stepped out in faith.

I drew parallels between the stamina I needed to break into modeling and what I needed for a powerful prayer life. I went to audition after audition and kept myself visible before casting directors and agents. Just like in prayer, I reasoned, if I pound on the door and ask enough times, it's bound to burst open eventually. Matthew 7:7 (NIV) says it well: "Ask and it will be given to you; seek and you will find; knock and the door will be opened to you. For everyone who asks receives; the one who seeks finds; and to the one who knocks, the door will be opened."

With these thoughts swirling in my mind, I made my way through the revolving doors of the Merchandise Mart, a commercial building located downtown on the Chicago River. The spring bridal market was to be held here that weekend. Buyers and store owners came from around the country to visit designer showrooms and select gowns for their stores. Some insiders told me the best way to find a job for the show was to go a day before the market opened and to let them know I was available. This impromptu audition was my gutsiest move yet.

As I waited for the elevator to take me up to the tenth floor, I smoothed out my windblown hair. *Okay, God, this is it. I really need You now. Please grant me favor and lead me to the right client. If You don't show up, I'm going to fall flat on my face. Thank You for going before me and opening up doors no man can close. In Jesus's name I pray.*

I took a deep breath and stepped into the elevator. As I made the ascent, I thought about the time I'd ridden my bike off a dock and into a lake at a summer cabin our family had rented in Minnesota. I was nine or ten years old, and my older brother Donny had told me, "Whatever you do, don't chicken out at the last minute. If you do, you'll hurt yourself. If you're gonna go for it, go all the way." With that encouragement, I'd pedaled as fast as I could down that dock, my wispy blond hair trailing behind me. My little green bike and I flew off that final wooden plank as high and as fast as I could get us. I shouted at the top of my lungs, "Do the Dew!" as I plunged into the lake. (Mountain Dew was famous for its commercials in the 1980s where they did extreme stunts on bikes and skateboards and shouted this line.)

I also reminisced about the time I'd followed my brothers' lead and jumped off the roof of our garage into our above-ground swimming pool. *If they can do it, why can't I?* That time, my brother Andrew coached me. "Make sure you run fast and get some good speed. Aim for the middle of the pool. You've got to clear the side, or you're going to be in a lot of pain." I summoned my courage and made the jump. And then I did it again and again, all summer long. I added crazy poses in the air as I jumped and pushed the envelope.

And now here I was, pushing the envelope again. What did I have to lose? Back then, not making it would have hurt. Now all I had to lose were my pride and a possible job.

I exhaled and stepped off the elevator, rehearsing my speech in my head. I thought of my friend's advice: "Walk in like you know exactly where you're going, and no one will question you." I quickly surveyed the situation. There were fifteen, maybe twenty showrooms. I started on one end of the floor and worked my way around, stopping in any room that had lights on and people inside. The rooms varied in size, but most held racks of dresses, a small stage or runway, and seating for at least ten people. Many also had a backstage area where the models could change.

I cautiously stepped into the first room. People were talking and getting dresses ready. A lady was steaming veils in the corner.

"Excuse me for interrupting. My name is Amy, and I'm a model here in Chicago. I just wanted to ask if you need any more models for the bridal market this weekend?"

The man closest to the door addressed me. "Thanks for stopping by, but we've already booked our models. Good luck."

I heard that same answer multiple times as I made my way around the tenth floor. My confidence was beginning to wane as I came to one of the last rooms on the floor. The man inside was having an animated conversation on his phone. Normally, I'd tell myself to forget it. He was busy on the phone and I wouldn't want to interrupt him. However, something inside me said, *Stop here. Ask this man. He will hire you.*

I stood a little taller and straighter and squared my shoulders. I smiled and walked through the door. The man on the phone smiled back at me and gestured toward his phone. When he hung up, he introduced himself as Paul and asked, "How can I help you out today?"

I gave him my speech about being a model and asked if he needed any help that weekend.

"I believe we could use another model," he said. "Why don't you try on a dress or two so we can see how they fit, and we'll go from there?"

"Sure," I replied cheerfully as I took the gowns he handed me and went to the changing area in back. I prayed the dresses would fit perfectly, and they did. I was elated when he said I had the job. It turned out Paul was the president of the company.

I worked for Symphony Bridal, not only that weekend but for many years to come, modeling at both the spring and fall bridal markets. It was always a fulfilling and enjoyable job. Buyers came from all over the Midwest, and we modeled the season's new dresses for them on a shortened runway. Models made quick changes in the back, each of us wearing ten or fifteen different dresses per show. We did this repeatedly throughout the day as different groups of buyers came in.

We worked hard, but the client provided lunch, the other models were kind, and Paul was a hoot. To top it off, he always paid us on the last day we worked.

The long days gave me experience and confidence. They also turned out to be great networking opportunities. I was able to help my friend Lee get work at the shows, and I also met June, who encouraged me to try out for the auto show. My risks were rewarded, and God continued to open key doors for me as long as I kept knocking.

Chapter 14

MET-Rx and an Abundance of Grace

Each experience, each challenge, each lesson will take you to the next dimension, building on what's already inside of you. Whether you know it or not, God's been prepping you for destiny before you were even aware that you had a destiny. God has been preparing you for what you are about to do all your life. You have had no wasted experiences.

T. D. JAKES

On a June morning in 2002, Eric and I drove together to the Milwaukee Speedway. My agent had arranged for us to work together on a promotion for General Nutrition Center (GNC). Eric joined me on jobs occasionally, when his schedule allowed. He was going to college, working at a coffee shop to get insurance benefits, and doing independent contractor projects as well. It was a busy season for us both.

I welcomed the warm sunshine and humidity with a smile as we made our way to the grandstand. I thrived on outdoor jobs since I had spent so many of my formative years in the woods. It felt like I was putting on a favorite pair of old blue jeans.

This job, I would realize later, was actually a divine appointment that would change the course of my modeling career forever.

Eric and I stood in the sweltering heat, breathing in the fumes of the NASCAR races, while handing out samples of vitamin C chews to the fans passing by. A few feet away, under a tent, three MET-Rx fitness models greeted fans, signed autographs, and snapped pictures.

MET-Rx, I learned, made protein supplements and powders. It's best known as the company that introduced meal replacement protein powders to the bodybuilding industry. MET-Rx was the main sponsor of the World's Strongest Man contest for a number of years. Their products are available in stores throughout the United States.

The girls came out periodically, and when they did, I stepped up to support them. "Come on over," I called to the fans, "and meet the fitness, models from MET-Rx. Get your picture taken." As men and women approached, I also handed them a bag of goodies from GNC.

Several race fans asked me why I wasn't one of the models signing autographs. I learned to laugh it off. "Good question. You never know, maybe I will be someday!"

MET-Rx hired fitness models to represent their brand. The models promoted the brand at various events, including bodybuilding, fitness and figure competitions. The company wanted people who were fit, hardworking, and engaging as well as attractive. Character, attitude, and integrity mattered.

After working in the heat all day, one of the models, Grace, pulled me aside. "I saw how hard you worked today. Thank you."

"You're welcome," I told her. "I enjoyed working with all of you here."

"I don't say this to everyone, but you really supported us and made our job easier. I want to help you get more work."

I could barely thank her before Grace continued. "I'm giving you the contact information for GNC and for MET-Rx. Let me know when you contact them, and I'll email them to highly recommend you."

"Thank you so much! This is one of the kindest things anyone has done for me!" As my words rushed out, I heard that still, small voice. *Never despise small beginnings.* It paid for me to work hard, because I never knew who might be watching or when I could be promoted.

When we got home, Eric encouraged me to follow up right away. The next business day, I emailed GNC and MET-Rx, and Grace sent messages as well, copying me so I could see her affirming words and recommendation.

Not long after, I heard back from MET-Rx. They asked me to work with Michellie Jones a professional triathlete from Australia, at the Mrs. T's Triathlon Expo in Chicago. Michellie was sponsored by MET-Rx, and my job was to assist her by handing out samples and engaging the crowd while she chatted with the triathletes and signed autographs.

When I was a triathlete in the 1990s, I had always dreamed of being sponsored by a big company like MET-Rx. While my back injury had ended that career, God was still opening doors for me. He was redeeming all things, and this was the first of many fulfilling work adventures I would have with MET-Rx.

Chapter 15

Ladies, Start Your Engines

And the day came when the risk to remain tight in a bud
was more painful than the risk it took to blossom.
ANAÏS NIN

The summer of 2002 was a pivotal time for me. I kept knocking on doors and striving to make modeling my full-time job. I continued to discover new aspects of the industry and enjoyed the diversity of it all. From auditions to print jobs to working the runway, I never got bored. I dabbled in some acting, went on fitness modeling jobs, and worked trade shows. I continued to step into jobs that seemed bigger than I could handle, and with God's help and favor, doors kept opening for me. Every day I met new people, and I learned to navigate the city and stretch my horizons.

I drove downtown one hot, sticky day in July and looked for a free parking spot on the street near the Omni Hotel. I didn't want to pay for the expensive hotel garage, especially since this was an interview and not a paid job.

Fortunately, I found a spot about two blocks from the Omni. I turned off the car and sat for a moment to collect my thoughts and pray. *Well, God, this is it. My fourth and final interview for the auto show. I pray You would bless me with favor and confidence as I interview with Porsche today. Eric and I really need this. Please go before me and make a way.*

With that, I jumped out of the car and made my way into the hotel. I took the elevator up to the lobby, where I met my agent and another lady I'd never seen before. Olga, my agent, greeted me. "I want to introduce you to Margery, one of the owners of Productions Plus." Productions Plus is an agency that staffs narrators and product specialists for automakers that exhibit at auto shows.

We exchanged pleasantries, and then an idea popped into my head. "Let me ask you, Margery, what do I need to say or do to land this job with Porsche today?"

I'm not quite sure where that boldness came from, but this was my last shot to get a contract with an automotive manufacturer. A retainer contract like that would take a lot of stress and pressure off of me, as it would provide a dependable monthly income. I could fill in my time with other modeling and acting jobs.

My friend June referred to auto show contracts as "golden handcuffs." Models were guaranteed a good paying, steady gig, including not just a day rate but also a per diem, travel, and lodging allowance, and even perks like dry cleaning. On the flip side, however, models often missed out on acting and modeling jobs when they were on the road working auto shows.

Margery seemed a bit surprised by my question, but then a smile spread across her face. She nodded in approval. "I'm glad you asked, and I appreciate your boldness. Here's my advice: Don't give pat answers when they ask you why you want to work for the company. Instead, answer with specific details about what you know about Porsche and their products.

All their cars are handcrafted in Germany, and great care is taken in assembling each part of the Porsche."

I was thankful I'd been studying the Porsche website. I could add some facts that I'd learned to her answer.

Margery continued. "And remember to be yourself. Too many people go in there and try to be someone they're not. They try to act impressive. Megan and the team at Porsche are looking for down-to-earth, approachable talent."

That was a relief. My personality is naturally warm and friendly. I could do this. I thanked her for her help.

As I was getting ready to take a seat, Olga added one last bit of advice. "I may lead some of the questions in the interview, but make sure that you look at Megan when you answer."

I nodded. "No problem. Thank you for the advice."

When I was called for my interview, I followed Margery's advice, and everything went smoothly. I talked to Megan about my upbringing in Minnesota and how I'd learned a lot about cars from my four brothers and my dad. I talked about my college degrees and managing the teen center. I mentioned a lot of what I'd learned from the Porsche website when they asked questions about the company. I felt very good about the interview when I left the Omni that day.

Megan told me she had to finish interviewing people around the country. In the end, she could only choose fourteen for the team. Olga said she would call in a few weeks and let me know either way.

August rolled around, and Eric and I headed to Bridgeman, Michigan, where he was speaking at a week-long youth camp. Eric's dad is a pastor, so occasionally Eric would share his testimony at youth groups or special events. This youth camp, though, was special. Eric and his family had gone there for years; in fact, his parents had met there as teenagers. Plus, Eric and I both had a heart for kids. So he was excited to be the main speaker for a whole week of camp. He asked me to minister alongside him, and I prepared a message to share in chapel as well.

One afternoon, some of the teens and I wrapped up our chores early, and we piled into my car and drove to the local strip mall to relax and hang out. The girls wanted to do some back-to-school shopping, and we were standing in the women's department of Old Navy, chatting and admiring the latest trends. My phone rang.

"Hey, I think this is a Michigan number," I told them. "I'd better take it." I swallowed hard and then answered the phone.

"Hi, Amy, it's Olga. Are you sitting down?"

"Well, no. Actually, I'm out at a store and there is nowhere to sit down." I knew I was babbling. "What's up?" My heart began beating faster in my chest.

Congratulations, you've been selected for the Porsche team! You'll receive a contract to work this fall if you say yes . . . and Porsche is very selective on who they choose."

I started jumping up and down right there in Old Navy. The girls looked at me excitedly, and they started jumping up and down too.

I quickly collected myself and tried to keep my breath even. "Yes, I would love to work for Porsche this season! I'm thrilled they chose me. Thank you so much."

Olga told me my Porsche training would begin in early September at the Porsche Cars North America headquarters in Atlanta, Georgia. The auto show season began at the end of October and went through April.

Some auto companies also sent their models to special events like ride-and-drives, state fairs, golf tournaments, or races. The year I started working for Porsche, they sponsored the Women's Tennis Association. The overall number of shows and working days varied, depending on the size of the automaker and how many people were on the team, but Olga assured me I would be guaranteed a minimum number of paid days when I signed the contract.

As soon as I hung up the phone, the girls and I embraced each other in a group hug and did a couple of moves like we were celebrating a touchdown in the end zone. It seemed like God was continuing to sew together my career like squares on a quilt. Each one had a unique design, and yet they all fit together perfectly. And all my big jobs seemed to come when I was focusing on Him and helping others.

Chapter 16

A Kindred Spirit

Friendship is born at that moment when one person says to another,
"What! You too? I thought I was the only one."
C. S. Lewis

"*Oma!* You're not going to** believe this," I shouted as I burst through the door of her townhouse. "I have so much good news, and I can't wait to tell you."

"Well, it sounds like you had a wonderful week at camp. I would love to hear more." Eric's grandmother got up from her chair and shuffled into the kitchen. She switched on the tea kettle while I pulled out two big mugs and the peppermint tea, which was our favorite.

I had grown close to Elsie Joob over the years Eric and I had been together, especially after she and her husband, whom we called *Opa*, moved from Colorado to Illinois. I often visited her. I loved to hear her stories about how they'd emigrated from Hanover, Germany to America just before Eric's dad was born.

As I prepped the teabags, I told her all about the events of the past week.

"Eric did a wonderful job speaking to the kids at camp, and they responded well to him. I had a chance to share one night at chapel, too, and it was really fulfilling. And I have some amazing job news—your prayers are being answered, Oma!"

"Oh, really. What do you mean?"

"Simi called me when I was at camp, and she asked me to help with the launch for the new Austin Powers movie. So I drove from Bridgeman to Chicago just to be on *Fox News in the Morning*. I got to dance with a couple of other go-go girls and Austin Powers to promote his new movie, *Goldmember*."

"Wow, that sounds like quite the opportunity! But you had to drive all that way for such a short time?"

"Yes. But that's not the big news." I told her about getting the Porsche contract.

"Well, that is wonderful! We've been praying for good jobs, and now you get to work for a fine German company." She set her hot tea down and smiled at me across the table.

"I know, it's pretty wild." I grinned at her. "Do people notice that my last name is German, or is it all you Germans praying for me?"

Oma smiled and listened as I rambled on excitedly. When I was done, she said, "I'm very happy that you are getting all this work. How does Eric feel about you traveling for the auto show?"

"He's totally for it. He's been encouraging me to step out into bigger things. Like he said, it's a one-season contract. If I don't like it, I don't have to go back the next year."

"I'm glad to hear you are on the same page. That is important in a marriage." Our conversation shifted to what she and Opa were doing.

Oma and I were kindred spirits. She was like the grandma I'd always wanted but never had. My own maternal grandmother died before I was born, and I never had a close relationship with my father's mother. But with

Oma, I made the forty-five-minute drive to visit as much as possible. We shared not only the history of our lives but our current struggles as well. Whenever I visited, we ended our time in prayer, and we pledged to pray for each other until we met again.

Her support for me was critical in the early years of my marriage and the early years of modeling. Plus, it seemed I was often with her, watering plants or running to the grocery store, when my agent would call to book me on another job. God continued to bless me.

Today, though, I was in a hurry. "I gotta scoot, Oma. I've been requested by a casting agent for an audition, and I need to get my hair done."

"Amy, you look beautiful just like you are. Come here, take my hands." She took my hands and closed her eyes. "Lord Jesus, bless Amy as she goes on her audition and grant her work that pays well and honors You. And continue to bless her marriage to Eric. Bless him as he studies hard in college. Thank you for this young couple. Watch over them and keep them safe."

"And Lord," I added, "please continue to bless and watch over Oma and Opa. Keep them healthy and strong. Keep Oma's back and hip from bothering her, and bless them with many wonderful friends and visitors to their home. Provide everything they need, comfort them, and let them know you are near. In Jesus's name, amen."

We squeezed hands a minute longer and smiled at each other. "You pray such wonderful prayers. I so appreciate you coming over here all the time and looking after me and Opa."

"Thank you so much, Oma," I said as I gathered my things to leave. "I'm so grateful for you, and for all your support and prayers too. I look forward to seeing you and Opa again soon. Bye, I love you!"

I made my way out the back door. I already couldn't wait to come back and hang out some more. *She sure is one special lady,* I thought as I hopped behind the wheel of my car.

Chapter 17

Ooh Baby, Baby

Start believing today that things
are going to change for the better.
JOEL OSTEEN

I drove into Chicago for the audition I'd told Oma about. I was trying out for a print job for Medela, a company that produced breast pumps. The casting agency was full of chubby-faced babies and their mamas. I was auditioning for the role of mom even though I only had credentials as a dog mom at that point.

I had to be very natural for this role, so I hadn't worn much makeup and my hair was soft and conservative. I'd kept my outfit simple, too, with a tank top and yoga pants. I signed in and turned in my comp card. Then I found a chair, set my stuff down, and ran my fingers through my hair. I said a quick prayer for favor and peace.

And then I heard, "Amy Jube, you're next." *If someone pronounces my name right, it will be a miracle.* It is actually pronounced Jobe, like Job in the Bible.

I took a deep breath and let it out slowly. *You can do this. Believe positive. You look amazing. You love babies. You have great favor here.*

I made my way onto the set, stood in front of the camera, and smiled at the photographer. One of the assistants handed me a card with my name and number on it. I held it up for the first shot so I could be identified later when they were making selections. In the business, they call it *slating.*

The photographer addressed me in a businesslike tone. "You can put the card down now. Okay, can you fold your arms and give me a relaxed smile?"

"Sure." I followed the photographer's direction and smiled with confidence into the camera.

"Great. Now I want you to turn to the right and hold your pose, please."

I turned right and did as he requested.

"Okay, now turn all the way to the left and hold your pose."

I continued to follow the photographer's instructions, and we wrapped up just a few minutes later.

"Thank you for coming in today, Amy. Let me ask, how comfortable are you handling babies? Are you a mom, or have you done a lot of babysitting?"

"I'm not a mom yet, but I have a lot of nieces and nephews, and I've held a lot of babies. Sure, I'm open and comfortable with babies." *I just hope they're not the extra fussy kind that spit up everywhere and are inconsolable. Okay, stop that. Don't talk yourself out of this job.*

"Thank you for having me audition today," I said with a bright smile. "Take care!" And with that, I walked off set and gathered my belongings. Auditions for print jobs were a strange animal. Whenever I thought they went well and I expected to get the job, I didn't. And whenever I thought that the audition didn't go so well, I ended up landing the job.

Well, that was kind of neutral, so you never know. Lord, thank You for continued favor with the photographer and everyone at Medela. I pray that I stand out and can book this job.

In the modeling business, they say you're successful if you land one out of ten jobs you audition for in print, and one out of twenty jobs on camera. I'm not sure if those stats are accurate, but they kept me going when I had to audition over and over again. I learned to face rejection and heard a lot of nos, but when the yeses finally came, I felt like I was on top of a mountain.

What drew me to this business? Am I a glutton for punishment, or do I have an adventurous streak that just won't quit? Probably a little bit of both. I have heard it said, the greater the risk, the greater the reward, and I saw that play out more than once in this business. I was thankful to have God on my side as my ultimate agent. He opened the doors that were meant for me and closed the doors that were not best. I simply had to trust Him with whatever results He brought me.

A few days after the audition, I got a phone call from my agent. "Medela chose you as one of their models for the calendar. Congratulations!"

Chapter 18

Lost in the City

*Whoever dwells in the shelter of the Most High will rest in
the shadow of the Almighty. I will say of the Lord, "He is
my refuge and my fortress, my God in whom I trust."*
PSALM 91:1–2 NIV

I was riding the high of landing the print job with Medela as I
cruised into the city again, eager to go on my next audition. I walked into
the studio with an extra bounce in my step and an extra notch on my belt. I
had some confidence built up. *Maybe I'm on a winning streak here!*

This audition ended like most others. We exchanged pleasantries, and
I had no idea whether I would be considered for the job. I said my usual
prayer of thanks and asked God for favor as I made my way to my car.

As I started the engine, I looked around and realized I had no idea
where I was. I couldn't even remember which way I had come from. I got
out my printed directions (this was before GPS and smartphones) and tried
to get my bearings. But when I pulled out into the street and turned the way

I thought I was supposed to go, nothing looked familiar. I had no idea how to get back to the expressway.

I was lost. Again.

I pulled up to a red light and stopped. The person in the car behind me laid on their horn, and panic rose within me. My temperature spiked, and my palms felt sweaty. The light was red, but the horn was blaring. I decided to turn right.

I looked up as I stepped on the gas and saw the sign: No Right on Red. *Shoot!* I was already making the turn.

A second later, bright blue and red lights flashed in my rearview mirror. A Chicago police officer was pulling me over. As I maneuvered to the side of the street, I realized I was near the Cabrini-Green housing project, which wasn't a safe neighborhood.

I rolled down my window, and a very angry officer walked up to me and started screaming. "What the hell are you doing? Did you not see the No Right on Red sign?"

"I'm so sorry," I tried to explain. "I didn't see the sign until the last minute. I'm lost and just trying to find the expressway."

The scowl stayed on his face as he stared at me coldly and swore some more. The officer showed not one ounce of compassion.

"License and registration," he demanded. I handed him what he asked for, but unfortunately instead of my license, I had a paper ticket. In Illinois at the time, if you received a speeding ticket, your license was confiscated until you paid your fine. Then your license was returned with a hole punched in it, a visible reminder of your indiscretion.

His laugh sounded evil. "Well, this explains a lot. You really don't know how to drive. Do you know that if I give you a ticket right now on top of this, you could get thrown in jail?"

Tears welled up in my eyes and spilled down my cheeks.

"Follow me. I'm taking you to the station down the street."

Meekly, I pulled out behind him and took in my surroundings. *I'm not in Minnesota anymore, and this is certainly not a place I want to be. I could end up in a cell with a drug dealer or gangbanger.*

By the time we got to the station, I was shaking. My tears flowed freely as I followed him into the building and to a counter where other officers sat and processed paperwork.

The policeman behind the counter talked to me in a gentle voice. "What's wrong? Why are you crying?"

I choked back sobs and told him, "I'm scared. That officer told me I could be thrown in jail here."

The man at the desk grimaced. He shook his head and glanced at the other officer behind the desk. They exchanged knowing looks.

"Look, don't let him bother you. It's not true. You will *not* be thrown in jail here." He glared over at the patrol officer. "Don't take it personally. It's his issue, not yours. I just need to finish processing this paperwork, and I'll send you on your way."

"Thank you." I was so relieved. "Can you please also help me figure out how to get back to I-90 heading west? This whole thing started because I was lost and accidentally turned right on red."

"Sure, I can do that for you. No problem. Everything's going to be okay."

What a crazy scenario! All because I turned right on red?

I eventually made it home safely. When I told my family and friends at church what had happened, a number of people told me to contest the ticket. "You need to let a judge know what happened to you. That's totally unacceptable behavior for a police officer."

I never wanted to see that man again, but I agreed. I didn't want him to treat someone else the way he'd treated me. Maybe I could find some closure by telling the judge my story and standing up to the one who'd abused me.

On my appointed court date, I made my way down to the Daley Center in Chicago. Eric had to work that day, so I went alone. I prayed the entire drive to the city that the whole thing wouldn't backfire and that the judge would know I was telling the truth. I prayed for favor, justice, and vindication.

In the courtroom, I sat nervously and waited for my case to be called. Finally, the bailiff called my name and case number. My heart started beating faster. They called the police officer's name. No one answered. They called it again. There was no sign of him anywhere. He was a no-show.

"Case dismissed!"

Because the police officer didn't show, I was cleared of all wrongdoing and didn't have to pay my ticket. He must have known he was wrong, and that's why he didn't show up. He knew the judge would rule in my favor.

As I left the Daley Center, it felt like the weight of the world had been lifted off me. I said a silent prayer of thanks to God for watching over me the day of the incident and for giving me favor that day in court. He continued to keep His promise to bless and protect me as I stepped out in the direction He was leading.

I determined not to let this incident dampen my spirits or keep me from going on future auditions and jobs.

Chapter 19

Hand from Heaven

*Relying on God has to begin all over again every
day as if nothing had yet been done.*
C. S. Lewis

I returned home from my Porsche training late in September of
2002. Our team had spent a week in Atlanta cramming a lot of knowledge
into our heads and topped it off with an eighty-question test to see what
we'd retained. I'd learned about all the Porsche makes and models, the
history of the company, and what made people so enthusiastic about the
brand.

My mind was still swimming as I made my way into the city and prepared
to work a double booking. My first job was a trade show, and after that, I
would go straight to a GNC store in the suburbs of Chicago. I was going
to work an event there for MET-Rx with Bill Kazmaier, former World's
Strongest Man.

I was excited and thankful to have plenty of work and a variety of jobs. But that particular day, I was also concerned. Before I'd left that morning, I'd tried to check the radiator on our Pontiac Sunfire. It was leaking, and I needed to keep checking fluid levels and add more if needed. But that morning when I went to open the radiator cap, it wouldn't budge. I tried everything.

Eric was out of town, and so the car and I were on our own. As I drove east on I-90 and the Chicago skyline came into view, I stepped up my prayers yet again. *God, I need Your help with this one. It's hot out here, and I have a lot of driving to do today. I need to get that radiator cap off to add fluid. Please send me some help.*

The trade show job went smoothly, and I made my way back out of the city to the GNC store. I continued to pray. I located the store, parked, and gathered the MET-Rx samples and gear that we were to give away.

Inside, I met Bill Kazmaier, a tall, extremely muscular man. Together, we set up our table near the front of the store. Bill would sign autographs and take pictures with people, and I would hand out samples of MET-Rx.

Things went smoothly, and a couple of hours later I was talking with some customers when I overheard Bill addressing the small crowd that had formed around him.

"Now, kids, watch this. Here's what happens if you drink your milk and your MET-Rx protein shakes and eat your broccoli. You'll have the strength to bend a pan just like this, and if you keep thinking positive and telling yourself you can do it, you can shape it into a whole new thing." Bill took a frying pan and bent the sides up, turning it into a wad of metal with a handle.

The crowd was impressed. A boy shouted, "How did you do that? Can I try it too?"

"Sure. But I want you to remember something. If you work hard and hit the gym and take care of yourself, you can do whatever you put your mind to. Here, give it a try."

The boy huffed and puffed, but he couldn't make that pan budge.

Bill encouraged him. "You've got to keep believing and working hard. Envision yourself reaching your goal. And pray and ask God for some help. You'll get there."

With that, he took a large iron bar, held it out horizontally, and bent both sides down to make a horseshoe shape. The audience responded with a round of applause.

After the crowd died down, I chatted with Bill. "That's impressive. I've never seen anything like that before."

"Thanks. That's years of training and hard work." Bill had won the World's Strongest Man competition three times and had set more strong man records than anyone else at that time.

"Congratulations!" I told him. "I'm glad I got a chance to work with you today. You're really great with the kids."

"Yeah, I have a heart for them. When I was young, I committed my life to Jesus Christ. I know He's the one who gave me strength and helped me accomplish all I have in life. Now I want to encourage young people to believe in themselves and do all God has created them to do too."

We talked awhile about how I was a Christian and how I'd worked with kids at the teen center. Bill smiled and told me to call him Kaz.

"So, Kaz, where do you live?"

"I live in a small town called Auburn, down in Alabama. I have a gym there called Kaz."

What a small world! "No way! I went to Auburn University, and I totally remember your gym. I used to see all these bodybuilders going in and out of there."

As we wrapped up the event at GNC, the thought hit me. *If anyone can get my radiator cap off, it's the world's strongest man who can roll up frying pans to look like hot dog buns. Maybe he's the answer to my prayer.*

"Kaz, can I ask you a big favor?" I explained my situation.

"Sure, I can help you out."

When we got to my car, Kaz really had to work to get the radiator cap off.

"I think it may have been screwed on crooked. Who put this on last? They must be pretty strong."

I grinned. "That would be my husband, Eric. I guess he is really strong!"

God had certainly heard my prayer that morning about needing help with my radiator cap, and He showed up big time. He sent me one of the strongest men in the world with a heart of gold to help me along the way. I stood there a moment longer, relieved and amazed at God's timing and provision.

Chapter 20

Sacrifice Pays Off

*You have not lived today until you have done something
for someone who can never repay you.*
JOHN BUNYAN

"You want to take *what* to Minnesota?"

"I want to take the VCR and my Tae Bo tapes. I called the hotel, and they don't have VCRs in the rooms."

"You need the VCR and your tapes for a few days with your family? Are you sure?"

I explained that since it was the holidays, I'd be indulging in more food, and I needed to keep fit. "What if I get called for a big job in January? I don't want to be all flabby."

"Whatever you say. You're the boss," Eric said with a twinkle in his eye.

We'd made it a tradition to spend Christmas in northern Minnesota with my parents, four brothers, their spouses, and a growing number of nieces and nephews. *At least there's no pressure on me to bring grandchildren.*

We enjoyed a white Christmas, and Eric and I stayed cozy together in our hotel. Between family gatherings, sleigh rides, and holiday get-togethers, I'd put on my workout clothes and get my cardio on in our room.

When January rolled around, I was thankful I'd made the sacrifice to work out.

"Are you ready to show your abs?" One of my agents asked me. "I have an audition for you at SPRI Fitness. They're looking for a female model for their ab ball box cover. You need to come in a sports bra and shorts, hair pulled back, and natural makeup. Let me give you the address."

A couple of days later, I walked into SPRI's corporate office in the northern suburbs of Chicago. I had a good feeling about the job. Everyone was friendly and personable. They reminded me of friends and neighbors back home in my small town. I worked out with an ab ball regularly, so I was comfortable doing the exercises, and I'd done an ab workout that morning, so my muscles looked especially defined.

The next day, my agent called to say I'd landed the job. In fact, I went on to work for SPRI several times. Not only did I get to be on their ab ball box cover, I also made it onto the cover of their catalog. One of the SPRI reps even gave me free equipment to help me stay in shape every year. They were one of my favorite print clients to work with in Chicago.

One day a few months later, Eric walked into the house with a big smile.

"Hey, you didn't tell me you were going to be on Oprah."

"What do you mean? I wasn't on Oprah."

"Well, maybe you weren't in person, but you were on the cover of the SPRI ab ball they had on the show. Someone at work told me they saw you."

That box really got around. Someone on the Porsche team mentioned they'd seen me in a TJ Maxx down in South Carolina too.

Not every job turned out that great. About the same time as my work with SPRI, my agent got me a fitness print job up in Milwaukee. It would pay well, and I was excited. I worked out and ate well as I prepared for the shoot. But then, about three days before the job, my agent called to say the client decided to cancel. There was no real explanation for why, and I had no contract to protect me.

I felt bummed out and frustrated that the job fell through, but God wanted me to think about something else. *Amy, remember this job is not about you. I called you here, and I will keep you here. I handpick every assignment for you, and I want you to focus on others. Share My love and help others along the way. As you are a blessing, you will be blessed in return.*

A short time later, I was back at my alma mater, Christian Life College, where I met a beautiful blonde who beamed like the sunshine. Not only was she physically attractive, but she had inner beauty too. She seemed to radiate as she smiled.

I introduced myself. "I started modeling a couple of years ago, and I think you could model too. You have a great look. Have you ever thought of being in the business?"

"Wow, thank you! I just came to the States recently. My parents were missionaries in Romania, and I grew up there. I'm interested in hearing more about modeling."

I gave Crystelle my phone number, and we began a series of phone conversations. I coached her on what I knew about how to get started in the business, from comp cards to agencies.

A few months later, I was sitting in the dentist's chair, waiting for the Novocain to kick in before yet another root canal. I was alone in the room when my phone rang.

Pick up the phone. You need to answer this call.

I jumped up and grabbed my phone before it could go to voicemail.

"Hi, this is Amy."

"Oh my gosh, I'm so glad you answered! I am sitting here at Ford, and I don't know what to do. I came to an open call to register, and they asked me to go exclusive! What should I do? Do I say yes?" It was Crystelle.

"Wow, congratulations! Ford is one of the best agencies in Chicago, so I think you should say yes. You are young, and if they asked you to go exclusive, I'm sure they'll find you work."

"Oh, thank you. I didn't know if it was the right decision. I'm so glad you took my call."

Crystelle has gone on to have a very successful modeling career, as have others I've helped over the years. Just as God was faithful to bring me helpers and open doors that were all a part of His design and master plan for me, He also used me to help others in the same way. God has truly been my agent.

Chapter 21

Breaking News

Men make history and not the other way around. In periods where there is no leadership, society stands still. Progress occurs when courageous, skillful leaders seize the opportunity to change things for the better.

HARRY S. TRUMAN

The first year I worked for Porsche, I found myself smack dab in the middle of a Detroit riot.

It was January of 2003, and the auto show season was ramping up. I flew from O'Hare to Detroit's Metro Airport and then took the People Mover train to my hotel. As we approached downtown, I felt like I was on a movie set from some sci-fi thriller. I saw block after block of abandoned skyscrapers and office towers frozen in time. They were broken down, shattered, and silent. Windows were blown out, and there was graffiti everywhere. It looked like a bomb had gone off, and no one had come back to clean it up.

It was a lot to take in. I'd heard that there had once been riots, and the city had never fully recovered. I felt a heaviness there, and it broke my heart. I've always had a soft spot for people and places that are down and out. I've worked through a lot of tough things myself.

I was broken, and God restored me, so why couldn't He restore the people and the city of Detroit? In my hotel room, I dropped to my knees and prayed for Detroit. I prayed that God would bring life, salvation, healing, and restoration to that place.

Then I called Eric. "You're not going to believe my first impression of this city. It's really sad. I can imagine how it was booming at one point."

"I've heard that," he said. "Remember to be careful there."

"Yeah, I know. Can you pray with me?"

"Sure."

Eric and I had prayed together daily since early in our marriage, whether we were at home or traveling. It helped us stay connected and kept God at the center of our relationship.

The next day, I took the People Mover to Cobo Hall, where I would work the North American International Auto Show, one of the largest and longest shows in the nation. The first week is a press preview, and important people come from all over the world to showcase the newest makes and models. All of Porsche's executives from their German headquarters, including the CEO himself, Dr. Wiedeking, were there.

All week, excitement filled our massive booth in a prestigious corner of the hall. The booth designers had gone all out—white glass tiles, shiny chrome, an upstairs balcony, a bar, and meeting rooms all surrounded the sleek, shiny 911s, Boxsters, and Cayennes. Flat-screen TVs showed Porsches driving on rocky bluffs near the ocean. By the end of the show, everyone on the Porsche team knew every note of the video's background music, which played in a loop. I even wrote my own lyrics to the song.

As press week wrapped up, the show opened to the public. We braced ourselves for two more weeks on the job.

I was new on the team, so I was still learning how the whole booth ran, as well as reinforcing my product knowledge and specifications for each car. Some of our cars were locked because they were so expensive, but we usually kept at least one open from each line. Customers could get in to touch and feel the Boxter, Cayenne, or 911. Product specialists like me helped manage the booth and kept things running smoothly. We were assigned to different areas in the booth like the front desk, a specific vehicle, or the poster bin, which we kept stocked with complimentary pictures of sleek Porsches that attendees could take home.

Porsche didn't use narrators on microphones to talk about new vehicles in their booth. They didn't feel they needed narrators to talk up vehicles that would sell themselves based on brand recognition and reputation. Instead, the product specialists made conversation with people in the booth. We carried around notecards for quick reference so we could inform and educate customers about the details of a car, as well as the history and heritage of Porsche.

I now understood why Porsche had let each product specialist test drive the different vehicles during our orientation. We could share with the public our own experiences driving the different models.

I showed up on Saturday afternoon with coffee in hand. Kathryn, a veteran on the team, and I were scheduled to work the second shift, closing the booth at night. I was a little nervous about that. Someone had told me that the first Saturday night of the Detroit show is a notorious gang night, when gang members show up and basically take over the place. Trouble always seemed to brew on Saturday night.

Sure enough, as the afternoon turned to evening, I noticed a shift in the atmosphere. The show floor seemed like a ghost town as far as workers were concerned. Many of the booth staff left early for their own safety. At the same time, there was a growing number of young people moving in big groups. They'd walk slowly down the aisles and give everyone the "stare down." I was feeling increasingly uncomfortable.

Around eight o'clock, the beefy security guard from Audi ran across the aisle toward us. His face was white, and his eyes were filled with alarm. "Girls, get the hell out of here. *Now!*"

"Why? What's happening?"

"Something's going down on the other side of the hall. It's chaos. You need to get out *now*. Grab your stuff and go!"

I was ready to bolt. I said to Kathryn, "Let's go!"

"No," she shook her head. "We have to wait for Todd. He told me not to leave here until he walks us out. It's not safe in here, but it's not safe out there, either." Kathryn's boyfriend worked at the Toyota booth.

God, please send Todd. I want to get out of here! Please protect us and get us to our hotel safely.

I froze as a rushing sound, like a stampede, surrounded us. Every hair stood up on the back of my neck. I don't know if I've ever felt that scared. It sounded like a herd of cattle running across a dusty terrain. Except it wasn't cattle. I heard people screaming and running toward us from the far side of the hall.

Is this a riot? Please don't let me die, God.

The noise and commotion continued to build as the mob moved from the south side of the hall, where the American cars were, to the north side, where Porsche and the other foreign cars were stationed.

I unglued myself from my frozen position and barreled as fast as I could toward the back of the booth. I didn't care if I was wearing a skirt and heels. I grabbed my purse and coat from my locker. *Can I just lock myself in this back room? Or should I take the chance and make a beeline for the door? I want to get out of here alive!* Todd finally arrived, jarring me from my catastrophic thoughts. The three of us scrambled out the nearby doors and into the lobby. People were running in every direction. Todd put one arm around Kathryn and the other arm around me, steering us through the crowd and out the front doors.

This chaos is even worse than Mardi Gras in New Orleans. My college trip to Louisiana was my only reference point for what was going on. Outside, Todd whistled for a taxi and said to the driver, "We need to get out of here fast."

As we settled into the cab, we struggled to catch our breath. It was only a six- or eight-block drive to our hotel, but once we stepped into the lobby, we all breathed a big sigh of relief.

"That was so scary. Thanks for looking out for me."

"That was nuts!" Kathryn said. "Go get some rest. We can talk about it more tomorrow. We need to talk to our agency and let them know what happened tonight."

I made my way to the elevator. *Thank you, God, for watching over me and protecting us all tonight. Thank you for sending Todd to help us. Please keep us safe the rest of our time here. Help me not to be afraid to go back there.*

As I walked off the elevator, my breathing started to slow and my heart stopped pounding. *Peace and quiet.*

In my room, I made sure the door was securely locked and plopped down onto my bed. I flipped on the TV in time to hear the newscaster say, "This just in. Moments ago, there was a stabbing right outside Cobo Hall."

I was just there. That could have been me. Thank You, God, for protecting me and keeping me safe tonight.

After I calmed down, I called Eric and told him everything that happened. "I know God opened the door for me to work for Porsche, but why did this crazy thing happen?"

"Just because God calls you to do something doesn't mean it will always be easy," he reminded me. "It doesn't mean you won't have problems. Trust that He brought you there, and because of that He will protect you and keep you there."

"I guess you're right. I just thought this would be better."

"Well, you didn't get hurt. He did protect you, and He will continue to protect you. Where He guides, He provides."

Reassured, I was determined to finish the job with a positive attitude. Every day I went straight to my booth, used the closest bathroom, and went straight back to my hotel at the end of my shift. I brought my lunch and ate it in our break room. Security guards told us that kids had rioted in Cobo Hall on Saturday night, and there was damage to the Ford and Chevy booths and vehicles. I never ventured anywhere outside our booth to survey the damage or find out what happened.

Just days after the episode, I received a promising phone call. I listened to my voicemail as I ate my lunch. "Hi, this is Lori calling from MET-Rx. We're interested in making you one of our sponsored athletes. We'd like to offer you a contract for 2003. Can you give me a call back and we can discuss the details?"

This was a dream come true. Even though my injuries had brought my triathlon career to an end, God was still faithful to grant me the desire of my heart: a contract with a big nutrition company.

I called her back immediately. "Yes, I'd love to accept your offer."

"Great." Lori sounded happy. "I'll get the contract sent to you right away. You'll be a fitness model/product specialist for our company. The contract will spell out the terms of our agreement. As soon as I have some dates for the next event, I'll let you know."

God was opening the doors big time. I walked around Detroit with a renewed joy during the rest of the show. He was keeping His promises and faithfully making a way for me. And I was determined to keep trusting even when things got a little sticky. I reminded myself that no place or job would ever be perfect this side of heaven.

Chapter 22

Closing Up the Club

When God gives you a new beginning, it starts with an ending. Be
thankful for closed doors. They often guide us to the right one.
A WOMAN OF FAITH

A couple of weeks later, I was working my hometown show. Although the Chicago Auto Show didn't have the fanfare and the full week
of press that Detroit did, it was still one of the best-attended shows in the
country. Most days, the floor was packed with people. The show tested
the endurance of everyone on the team.

In addition to working the show, I'd booked a runway gig at a
nightclub. I'd done several of these shows in Chicago before. At this
show, the models would wear swimsuits under fur coats provided by a
local Chicago furrier. It was an interesting combination, but I worked
with my friend Lee, which made it more fun.

It was frigid that week, and a couple of recent tragedies were hitting
close to home for everyone. Just a couple of blocks from McCormick

Place, some security guards at the E2 nightclub had sprayed pepper spray to break up a fight, and it had caused a stampede for the door. Twenty-one people had been killed. Then just a couple of nights later, the band Great White was performing at The Station nightclub in Rhode Island. Faulty pyrotechnics set the stage walls and ceiling on fire, and the place had gone up in a blaze. One hundred people lost their lives in that fire, and more were injured while trying to escape.

Now here I was, preparing to go to a club. I couldn't shake the heavy feeling inside of me. *Don't go in there.*

I talked to my agent about my concerns, and she reassured me that the club owners were taking extra precautions. They wouldn't allow the club to fill beyond capacity. Still, I didn't trust nightclubs, and I didn't want to be in one. At the same time, I didn't want to call off the job at the last minute, and neither did Lee. It was a tug of war inside of both of us.

We decided we would pray and partner up and tackle the job together.

As soon as I got to the club, I found the emergency exits. I wanted to know my ways of escape. I still didn't feel completely at peace, but thankfully our holding/changing area was near an exit. God had our backs.

Lee and I made it through the show. We both turned down the shots of liquor that the bartenders offered us. I wanted to be aware of my surroundings, especially there. I kept my fur coat on the whole time I worked the runway. It was the middle of winter, and I didn't want to walk around with my white skin glowing in a bikini. And truth be told, I didn't feel comfortable walking around the stage in just a bikini in front of that crowd of partygoers.

As soon as the show ended, Lee and I changed back into our regular clothes, collected our paychecks, and said our goodbyes. We made it out without issue or incident, but when we reached the parking lot, I said, "That's it for me. I'm done with these club shows. I don't feel safe here. I'm going to stick to modeling jobs in more positive places."

Lee nodded. "I hear you. I enjoy working with you, but this isn't the best place for either of us."

As I drove home, I cried from exhaustion over the long hours I'd worked at the auto show, and I cried tears of relief that I made it out of a nightclub alive after those two catastrophes in the other clubs.

God, I'm sorry. I don't know if I should have done this job. I'm done with these. He had opened the doors to these runway jobs, but maybe it was just meant to be for a season. One door was closing, but I trusted that He would open better doors for me along the way.

Chapter 23

Blackout Blessing

When you are tempted to give up, your breakthrough
is probably just around the corner.
JOYCE MEYER

Lee and I sipped our coffees and commiserated about the slow work season. It was the dog days of August, hot and humid, and the work was coming in as slowly as people walked on the sidewalk just outside the Starbucks window. Everything seemed to be dragging.

"Lee, what if we pray for each other to get some work? Maybe we can even book a job together. Did you send your stuff to MET-Rx yet?"

"Yes, they said they'll let me know if there are any demos or other jobs in our area. I told them we make a great team."

"Sweet! I'll mention something to them too. If they have jobs that require travel, we could always room together to cut down on costs. I hope some big jobs open up for both of us!"

"From your lips to God's ears. I could use a job this month."

As soon as those words came out of her mouth, my cell phone rang. The caller ID said Productions Plus.

"Hello? This is Amy."

"I'm so glad you answered." It was Olga, my agent. "We're in a bind here. I don't know if you heard, but there was a major blackout in Detroit this morning. Everything's shut down, including the airports. We have girls who were supposed to fly to Chicago for the Cayenne Ride-and-Drive Experience, and I don't think they can get there on time. Please tell me you're available to work this weekend."

"Sure, I can work this weekend. Thanks for thinking of me."

"Fabulous! Do you happen to have a girlfriend who's looking for some work too?"

I laughed out loud. "You're not going to believe this. I'm sitting here with my friend Lee right now, and we were just talking about work. This is literally an answer to prayer."

"Great, you're both booked. Can you get to the site by three this afternoon? It's in the southwest suburbs."

And with that, Lee and I gave each other a congratulatory hug and headed to our respective homes to prepare for the Porsche Cayenne Ride-and-Drive. The event was an invitation-only experience, where Porsche owners and other VIPs could test drive the new Cayenne on street and off-road tracks..

There was never a dull moment in this business. God knew exactly what we needed and when we needed it.

Lee and I arrived at the event that afternoon, which was set up in a large parking lot. Porsche had built test-drive areas, including one with cones in the shape of a figure eight and another with mounds of dirt.

We headed inside the big white hospitality tent, where we received our wardrobe for the day: burgundy sweater sets, khaki pants, and white gym shoes. We met the driving instructors and staff and then got to work. Since I had experience as a product specialist, I worked the main counter, checking in the guests and answering questions about the Cayenne. Lee handed out giveaways at the T-shirt counter.

The weekend went smoothly. Guests took turns taking the Cayenne out for a test-drive, collected Porsche swag, and met the driving instructors—former race car drivers who now worked at the Porsche Sport Driving Experience in Alabama.

Lee and I were grateful for the work, even though the hours were long. God certainly answered our prayers that weekend. No sooner had we spoken them, when the answer came. He never ceases to amaze me.

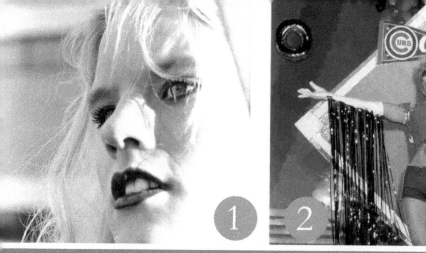

1 SARAH'S WINNING PICTURE
Sarah Burval Hansen's award-winning picture from her photography class at Oakton. Ironically, this is my "bad side" that shows my birthmark. This is an early sign that I am on the right track in pursuing a career in modeling.

2 MRS. ILLINOIS PAGEANT
On stage modeling my Chicago Cubs costume at the Mrs. Illinois Pageant. I didn't win but I did land a half-page spread in the Daily Herald, and I met one of my best friends!

3 FIRST PHOTO SHOOT
First photo shoot at Dan Duverney's studio in Chicago. This is the winning headshot, and I put it on the front of my first composite (comp) card.

4 FIRST PHOTO SHOOT WITH ERIC
Eric joined me halfway through the photo shoot, and Dan captured us together as a couple. I added this lifestyle shot to the back of my comp card.

As Marilyn Monroe for Sebastian at Midwest Beauty Show

Amy Joob

SIEMENS

Instant. Access. Anyware.
e.soft—Nuclear Medicine Workstation

5 MARILYN MONROE

Marilyn Monroe for Sebastian at Chicago's Midwest Beauty Show. I had my hair bleached platinum at this show, and I had never put color in my hair before. I drove home and cried.

6 SIEMENS

First print job for Siemens Nuclear Medicine. I showed up with my hair too puffy, and they really combed it down. My hands were too "veiny," so I had to hold them up in the air for about five minutes before I put them down on the keyboard for the shoot. Learned a lot of lessons that day!

7 RUNWAY AT DALEY CENTER

Modeling on the runway at Daley Center in Chicago for Strut Productions. Trying to lose my signature smile and put on a fierce look for the runway.

8 RECORD-BREAKING EVENT FOR GNC

World-record-setting day! James Thompson held all of us and jumped rope a number of times to set a world record. We all weighed over 450 pounds, and I don't know how we all managed to stay wrapped around him while he jumped!

9 MILWAUKEE JOURNAL
Spring Fashion Editorial for the *Milwaukee Journal*. Even I was surprised when I received the call. I did a lot of young mom and fitness print. I enjoyed the change as we modeled a number of fresh looks for the paper.

10 HARLEY DAVIDSON
Modeling Harley Davidson apparel at the annual dealer meeting in Milwaukee. I enjoyed wearing all of the leather and interacting with people. I started realizing more and more my favorite jobs involved entertaining and interacting with people.

11 MEDELA
Cozying up to a baby for the Medela Calendar photo shoot. It was harder than I thought–lots of people, cameras, and hot lights on set. I was trying not to break a sweat while looking natural and relaxed and praying the baby wouldn't cry.

LADIES SPORTSWEAR

THIS ISN'T JUST FASHION. IT'S HISTORY.

Our Ladies Sportswear Collection is full of new styles and classic favorites that will help your customers start the next 100 years off right. You can't miss out new Reflective Flame sleeveless Black T with embroidery and reflective trim. Another shining addition is the new Silver Pin, featuring rhinestones around the collar which are sure to both catch attention and sparkle sales. Also new is Harley Wings, which is a black, front zip sleeveless T with a textured, heat transferred appliqué. Back by popular demand are Scratch, H-D Dimensional, Stepping, and Whish Type.

Sizes S - 2X
35-HA00941 Mini B&S
Black Funnel-Neck Sleeveless T

Sizes S - 2X — **EMBROIDERED**
36-HA00959 Embroidered Flame
Black with Orange V-Neck Cap T

Sizes S - 2X
37-NA00961
Steel Hooded Slee

12

SPRI

13

PROFESSIONAL FITNESS PRODUCTS CATALOG

Phone 800.886.4759   Fax 800.536.5850   www.holoubek.com

12   HARLEY DAVIDSON DEALER MEETING

Modeling Harley Davidson apparel for their catalog in Milwaukee. I found this job pretty easy as I liked the clothes and how they looked on me. I could see myself buying and wearing some of these outfits as they were cute and sporty.

13   SPRI CATALOG

13.5   I did a few jobs with Spri and enjoyed working with everyone at this company. They were kind, friendly, and encouraging. I was right in my element. I was so excited when I received a copy of the catalog and discovered I made the front cover! I was also featured on a SPRI ab ball box cover at a later shoot.

14   ARIANNA 3 MONTHS

Arianna's baby picture at three months old. She is wearing my outfit in pale pink that I also wore as a baby. People commented to me that she looked like the Gerber baby.

LANCE &
ABILITY

13.5

14

ROLLERS

ffective balance and alignment tool for developing core stabilization, balance and stamina, and body awareness. May also be used for ching and self-mobilization of joints and spine. Begin with the ball- and progress to more difficult full-round roller. Choose either lengths based on body type and activity. Select 6-inch (easier), nore difficult) diameter roller based on ability level. One free Chart per order.

may be combined for a quantity discount

	FR-124	FR-126	FR-364	FR-366	HR-124	HR-126	HR-364	HR-366
	12"	12"	36"	36"	12"	12"	36"	36"
	4"	6"	4"	6"	4"	6"	4"	6"
	Full	Full	Full	Full	Half	Half	Half	Half
				Price Each				
	$7.50	$7.95	$15.95	$16.95	$7.50	$7.95	$10.95	$11.95
	7.00	7.50	14.95	15.95	7.00	7.50	10.50	11.50

l Charts Available   Item# FR-C . . . $ .25 ea.

FOAM ROLLER KITS
Item# FR-KIT . . . $43.95
Includes all 4 full rollers.
Item# HR-KIT . . . $33.35
Includes all 4 half rollers.

ESSORIES &
UCATION

NEW!
XERDISC™
An advanced balance training tool for single leg exercises. Use two Xerdisc™ products for double arm or double leg strength and stabilization activi- ties. This lightweight, portable 13-1/2"D x 2-1/2"H air-filled disc can be inflated for less of a balance challenge and deflated to provide more of a balance challenge. One free Instruction Chart per order.
Item# XD-B

Quantity	Price Each
1-9	$25.00
10+	24.00

Additional Instruction Charts
Item# XD-C . . . $ .25 ea.

™ BOARD
compliment to the Xerdisc™. Place on lic™ and instantly convert your disc into oard. This 15" round board is also in aining aid for newly introduced Xerdisc™ quiring less of a balance challenge.

NEW!
VHI FOAM ROLLER CARD KIT
This complete collection of foam roller exercises is ideal for developing core stabilization, balance, mobi- ization, movement awareness and much more. These 4-1/2" x 5-1/2" exercise resource cards are designed for fitness instructors, personal trainers and rehab

NEW!
BOOSTING YOUR METABOLISM VIDEO FEATURING THE SPRI™ XERDISC™
with Jim Karas
This 30 minute video uses the SPRI Xerdisc™. This is the first video to specifically demonstrate 10 effective exercises for the upper body, lower body and your abdominals. The Xerdisc™ is easy to use, fun and effective for both weight loss and toning your muscles.

19 MARIUSZ PUDZIANOWSKI
World's Strongest Man Mariusz Pudzianowski and I working together at Club Industry in Chicago.

20 MARKETPLACE HANDIWORK OF INDIA
Print modeling for the Marketplace Handiwork of India catalog. I enjoyed being on set as they had a great hair and make-up artist. I wore several different looks and worked with women from many different cultures.

21 BLAIR HOUSE
Arianna "speaking" at the Blair House as we toured there with Walter and Carrie. We had a fulfilling time together as a family in Washington, DC.

22 ARIANNA AND OMA
Hanging out with Oma at her place in Del Webb. She loved when we came to visit, especially with Arianna.

BLAIR HOUSE
Washington, D.C.

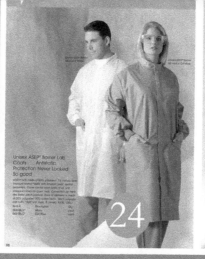

23

Sahaara
IRIT   STYLE   SUBSTANCE

24

25

(23) **SAHAARA CATALOG**
Informal Modeling at an East Indian event, and we made it into the Sahaara Catalog.
One of the many jobs I got through Simi and Strut Productions.

(24) **MEDLINE**
One of several print jobs I did for Medline, a global medical supply manufacturer and
distributor. They became a recurring client, and the studio/crew was always so kind to me.

(25) **PHOTO SHOOT WITH GEORGE VINCENT**
Another photo shoot with George Vincent. He helped me with several of my comp
cards over the years, and we included Eric and Arianna in pictures too.

(26) **IMTS FOR TIGER TECH TOOLS**
The eye of the tiger became a reality as I worked for Walter at the IMTS tradeshow.
We did live tiger shows several times a day throughout the week.

26

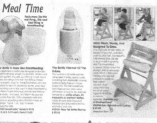

Meal Time

27 ONE STEP AHEAD CATALOG

Playing a young mom and modeling for One Step Ahead Catalog. On this photo shoot the first toddler didn't cooperate and they had to call in a new model. We were delayed almost two hours because they did not have a back up on site.

28 ARNOLD CLASSIC

Working with World's Strongest Man competitor Jesse Marunde as well as fitness models Lee and Natalie at the Arnold Classic.

29 PORSCHE TRAINING

Porsche training at the racetrack–one of my favorite days of the year! I am standing (my hand is on the hood) with the team from across the U.S. as well as our instructors who are professional race car drivers. A taste of heaven!

30 WORKING WITH STARLIGHT

Working a tradeshow at McCormick Place with my friend and big sister in the business, Deb, AKA Starlight. McCormick would eventually become my home away from home!

31 AT RENNSPORT REUNION WITH HURLEY HAYWOOD

Working and sneaking in a little bit of racing at Rennsport Reunion in Daytona. Learning to drive from Hurley Haywood was amazing. It was my birthday weekend, and the guys from Porsche let me take a car for a spin!

32 LIME ROCK RACES FOR PORSCHE

At the ALMS races in Lime Rock, Connecticut, for Porsche. It was a picturesque track set in a valley with plush trees all around. Our two RS Spyders kept coming in first and second, and I had to pinch myself at times to realize I wasn't dreaming.

33 HOT SPOT AT HOME FOR T-MOBILE

Hanging out with my favorite cell phone—Eric! Working an activation for T-Mobile entitled "Hot Spot at Home." I had the ruptured cyst on my ovary during this job and spent a day in the ER. I realized during this job that my true, desired hot spot was at home with Eric and Arianna.

34

MEETING JOEL OSTEEN
Meeting Joel Olsteen with Danette at Lakewood Church when we worked the Houston Auto Show. He encouraged me to follow my dream of speaking and writing. It was one of the most welcoming churches I have ever visited.

MEETING CHRISTIE BRINKLEY AT THE HAMPTON CLASSIC
Meeting Christie Brinkley on the final day of the Hampton Classic. She is warm and friendly--a beauty inside and out!

STERLING TRUCKS
Sterling Silver Girls working for Sterling trucks at a tradeshow. Fun to wear something unique, but my goodness the silver spandex is unforgiving!

35

36

200

ME AND ERIC IN HAWAII
Eric and I on a day off from the Honolulu Auto Show. I'm thankful we got to spend some downtime together during a busy work season.

MEETING COLIN POWELL
Eric and I working production for Accenture at the Q-Center and meeting Colin Powell —one of the best motivational speakers we have ever heard!

39 FAMILY FOOTBALL
Are you ready for some football? The Joob Family says, "Bring it!" Picture taken courtesy of our friend Sylver McAllister.

40 MEETING TED DIBIASE
Hanging out with Ted Dibiase at Ascension Convention at the Rosemont Hyatt. I spoke several times at breakout sessions and supported the youth conference put on by Christian Life College.

41 ADAM AND JOANNA'S WEDDING
All of us helping out at Adam and Joanna's wedding in Duluth. So happy for my brother Adam and his new bride, JoJo!

42 FAMILY CHRISTMAS PIC 2018
Me, Arianna (13), Ashton (9), and Eric are celebrating the season and His goodness as we look forward with anticipation to seeing dreams fulfilled in 2019!

Chapter 24

Bodybuilding Buddies

*I love my work. We have some good times here, and
they take care of me. This is my extended family here,
and I look forward to each day coming in.*
DORTHA CHAPMAN

A tidal wave of work flooded in during the fall of 2003. I renewed
my contract with Porsche and was promoted to lead product specialist. I
attended another training week in Atlanta, where I got to enjoy driving
Porsches at the racetrack this time around.

Back home I received a call from US Nutrition, the parent company
of MET-Rx, Pure Protein, Nature's Bounty, Balance Bar, Body Fortress,
and more. They asked if I would be interested in promoting MET-Rx at
some Vitamin Shoppes in and around Chicago. I welcomed the additional
opportunity.

I was riding a high. I was blessed to have my work with Porsche, and
everyone at MET-Rx so far had been amazing. My MET-Rx contact, Lori,

and I had especially connected. We'd both grown up and had family in Minnesota, and we shared a passion for running. I wanted to do a good job for her and for all of them. It helped that their products fit my personality and athletic background completely.

I booked a MET-Rx event at the Vitamin Shoppe in Lincoln Park, Illinois. Once again, I was working with one of the world's strongest men, this time it was Mariusz Pudzianowski.

At the nutrition store that day, I introduced myself to the manager and set up the MET-Rx display on the table the store provided. We had a special tablecloth and signage, as well as lots of bite-sized samples of bars. Once the event began, I'd also pour protein shake and energy drink samples.

Just before the event was scheduled to begin, Mariusz walked in. He was tall, with a definite presence. His neck, shoulders, and biceps were all huge. He wore a buzz cut and had piercing blue eyes. He looked focused and determined as he walked over to the table with another man.

We introduced ourselves. Mariusz told me he lived and trained in his hometown in Poland but traveled throughout the United States doing events and shows for MET-Rx. He didn't talk much, and his thick accent made me feel like I was talking to Arnold Schwarzenegger's character in *The Terminator*.

The man with Mariusz introduced himself as Tom. Tom seemed to be the spokesperson for the pair. He engaged me and the customers more. Together, the three of us made a good team, and people seemed excited to meet Mariusz and sample our new bars and shakes.

The following month, Mariusz and Tom were back in Chicago for the Club Industry trade show at McCormick Place, which Lee and I both worked. The event featured everything a business owner would put into a health club, including exercise equipment, fitness apparel, supplements, and more. Companies showcased everything from aqua pods that measured body fat to the latest exercise-tracking technology. Attendees could join in a spin or yoga class or try out the hot new exercise of the moment.

Lori stationed me at the center kiosk. "I'm going to have you work here next to Mariusz. He'll sign autographs, and you can scan people's badges so that we get each attendee's information for follow-up later. You can hand out samples too."

"Sounds good. I'll start chopping the bars and getting ready."

Mariusz came over, and we exchanged pleasantries. I noticed he was a little more talkative this time. Tom was still there, but he was more hands off. During the quieter moments of the show, I asked Mariusz about his life. He told me he trained for the strength competitions at home, with just his father and his brothers.

"That's cool." I was half joking when I asked him, "So you just pick up a huge boulder in your backyard and carry it across the lawn?"

His answer surprised me. "Yes, I do."

"And do you park in your backyard and practice pulling it with ropes?"

"Yes, that is what I do."

He explained his training to me and how he set up each of the World's Strongest Man competition events on his property.

"No wonder you're so good at what you do. You go in completely prepared." I was impressed.

Toward the end of the show, Lori suggested we all go out to dinner. "Amy," she said, "your birthday is coming up. We'll go out to celebrate. Where do you want to go?"

We decided on a sushi place in the River North neighborhood of Chicago. That night, we all got to know each other better, and over time the MET-Rx team became like family. Lori and Teresa from MET-Rx continued to send me on amazing jobs, and Lee became like a big sister to me as she encouraged me through various phases of life. Gary, a MET-Rx employee I met at a trade show, helped Eric and me find a great mortgage company when we bought our first townhome. And when I was pregnant with Arianna and struggling with the weight gain, Mariusz was right there, encouraging me to eat healthy and focus on the baby. "You'll get your figure back later. Right now, the health of the baby is most important."

I was well taken care of by MET-Rx, and I treasure the opportunities and the relationships I built while working for the company over a span of fifteen years.

Chapter 25

Help Is on the Way

*Real integrity is doing the right thing, knowing that
nobody's going to know whether you did it or not.*
OPRAH WINFREY

The auto show season picked up in November. By now I was
thoroughly enjoying traveling to cities across America, especially since I
felt increasingly comfortable with my Porsche product knowledge. This
was my first year as a lead product specialist, and I welcomed the added
responsibility and the pay raise.

As members of the Porsche team, we all had to take the same monthly
online tests as the dealership salespeople to make sure we kept up with
current information. Since they told us we were allowed to collaborate
on the tests, I made sure to find out who the sharpest salespeople were
across the United States, and then I'd call one of them if I was stuck on a
question. In hindsight, they probably didn't appreciate me interrupting
their day, but they were always willing to help.

Between auto shows I continued to model for the bridal market and squeeze in some runway and print jobs, character work (dressing up in costumes and going to parties or events to entertain people), and trade shows. With my work for MET-Rx as well, I was busy. My thirties could best be described as my workaholic years. I often worked twelve days straight and crammed in double bookings whenever I could. I was energized by the crazy pace.

Eric was just as busy. He was still going to college and working at a coffee shop for our insurance. He also did side jobs for our brother-in-law, Alex, who had started a lighting and production company, and for his good friend Jared, who did home construction projects.

In the middle of all this, my agent called. "Amy, I got you a fabulous print job. You've been selected by Miller Lite to be their girl for this season. They want to take pictures and make a life-sized cardboard cutout of you and put you up in stores throughout the Chicago area. They'll have you in shorts and a half T-shirt, like an NFL cheerleader. It will be tasteful. Isn't this exciting news?"

I swallowed hard. *How do I answer this, God? On the one hand, I'm thrilled and honored they chose me. It sounds like a fun job, and I would get great exposure. On the other hand, I decided long ago not to do any alcohol-related jobs. This goes against my convictions. I can't do this. I lead the ladies prayer breakfast each month at Christian Life College. God, give me the words to say.*

"I'm so sorry," I told the agent. "I can't accept. I'm honored they chose me, but this job doesn't line up with my convictions. I can't promote alcohol. Unfortunately, there have been a lot of issues with alcoholism in my family, and I don't want to be the one out there promoting it."

My agent was disappointed. She told me I was "blowing a big opportunity," but she accepted my decision and said she would find someone else. When we hung up, I started to worry.

I hope I didn't just burn a bridge with this agent, God. I pray she will keep me in mind for other projects and You will honor me for keeping my convictions.

Not long after, the test came again. Another agent called me. "I have wonderful news. You and one other person are being considered for a billboard. This is a huge job with a big buyout. You'll make a big bonus on this one, not to mention your face all over Chicago!"

I was excited. "This sounds fabulous! Tell me more. Who is the job for?"

"It's for this big vodka company out of Scandinavia. You have the perfect Nordic look for this, Amy. Please tell me yes. I think they're leaning toward choosing you."

Oh man, this really stinks. I had been dreaming of getting a billboard job, but I couldn't say yes. I had a sinking feeling inside me as I deliberated. In the end, my conscience won out.

"I'm sorry. This is probably one of the best job opportunities I've ever been offered, but I can't do it." I explained my convictions.

This agent was as surprised as the last. "I can't believe you would turn this down. But I don't want to pressure you to do something you don't feel right about either. I just hope you don't change your mind later."

Am I committing career suicide here? Maybe. But my goal had always been to stick to my convictions and to honor God, no matter what came my way. He had opened so many doors for me, and I felt so blessed to be modeling successfully this late in life. I wanted to have peace about every job I accepted.

Those were my thoughts as February rolled around again, and with it the Chicago Auto Show. We had a strong team all around, with twelve women from across the nation. I headed into the show rested. I hadn't been sent to the Detroit show that year, so I had more strength from the beginning.

We were a couple of days into the show, and it happened to be Valentine's Day. I worked the 10:00 a.m. to 6:00 p.m. shift, and the plan was for Eric to meet me downtown when I was done working so we could go out to dinner. We were long overdue for a date.

However, as I set up the booth that morning, I got a call from one of the evening-shift girls. She was sick and couldn't come in. Then another girl called to say she was incapacitated and couldn't work. A short time later, Patti rolled in for her shift, but she didn't look good. She tried to work for a while but ended up lying down in the break room. We were down to two product specialists working the floor when we usually had four or five. Especially in big cities like Chicago, we needed extra help on the weekends when it was busiest. I knew one additional person was coming in for the 2:00 to 10:00 p.m. shift, but that was the whole staff.

I called my agent to share the news. "As soon as I can, I'll come over there to help you sort this out," Carly said. When she arrived, we looked at the schedule together to figure out how to make it work. "We have a volunteer coming in from the Porsche Club of America. Maybe he can fill the poster bin."

"Okay, that sounds good. We'll see if he can help you with that. Still, it looks like you normally have four on the floor in the afternoon and evening. Do you think you can work a double today? We can pay you for your extra hours."

I reluctantly called Eric on my next break. "I have some bad news." I told him about the flu outbreak. "The agency asked me to work a double. I'm sorry I can't go out, but will you still come down and have dinner with me somewhere in the convention center?"

He agreed. "Since I'll be downtown anyway, I could stay and help out. At least we'll still be together."

Thanks to our volunteers we made it through the show that night, but it was exhausting. Porsche intrigued people. They wanted to see and

Chapter 26

New Addition

Lots of people want to ride with you in the
limo, but what you want is someone
who will take the bus with you when the limo breaks down.
OPRAH WINFREY

In the summer of 2004, I wasn't feeling quite right. I'd run a marathon in Anchorage, Alaska, earlier that summer, but that wasn't the issue. After getting some insight from Lee, I took a pregnancy test. To my shock, it was positive.

That same day, I received a phone call from my friend Kelly. "I have some amazing news to share with you," she said. "I'm pregnant!"

I was happy for Kelly and her husband, Nick, as I knew they had been trying to have a baby for a while. And then it hit me. The timing could not have been more perfect.

God answered my prayers! I asked God to send me a pregnant model friend, and here she is.

Kelly and I both lived in the northwest suburbs of Chicago, although we'd actually met in Tampa. We both worked the auto show circuit, but Kelly worked for Cadillac. We'd hit it off right away.

A few weeks later, once Eric and I had time to process our news and tell our families, I met Kelly at a local bakery. We sipped decaf coffee and noshed on some scones, and I finally had the chance to divulge my own secret to her.

"Congratulations!" She was smiling from ear to ear. "I'm so glad we can go through pregnancy together. God knew we needed each other. When is your due date?"

"The doctor told me February 21."

"Oh my gosh, my due date is February 26. What if we have these babies on the same day? They'll be birthday buds!"

As the months passed, we continued our regular breakfast and lunch dates, and we watched each other grow bigger and bigger. It was nice to take a break from constant dieting and watching our figures and comforting to eat whatever we wanted. We compared notes through each phase of the pregnancy. We prayed for each other to find the right work opportunities too.

Since I wouldn't be able to travel for a while, I got a part-time job as a recruiter for John Robert Powers (JRP) modeling school. I'd go into elementary, middle, and high schools all around Chicago and the suburbs giving motivational talks to students on a variety of topics like self-esteem, interviewing skills, careers in modeling and acting, and bullying. At the end of each talk, I would plug the school to see if any students were interested.

One January morning, I had to drive through a snowstorm to a Catholic school in the southwest suburbs. I had talks scheduled throughout the day, but as I stood in front of one of the classes, I felt unusually winded. *Why can't I catch my breath? What is wrong with me?*

My due date was about six weeks away, so I reasoned that it was just my size and the baby pushing on my rib cage. I made it through the day but questioned how much longer I could work.

Most modeling jobs were out of the question, but I did fly to North Dakota late in the pregnancy for a MET-Rx job, where I helped train and assist a new employee at a college event. Lori and the team were always looking for ways to help support me and my growing family.

After that, though, I was forced to rest. One of my agents said, "Enjoy the peace and quiet while you can. As soon as the baby comes, your world will be turned upside down. You won't get good sleep or rest for a while."

I tried to heed that advice, but I felt restless and couldn't get comfortable no matter how I lay or sat. Our little girl would be on the way soon, and I was ready to have her.

We certainly had enough stuff for her. Eric's parents had hosted a huge baby shower for us, and our family, friends, and church members provided abundantly for us and for our new little baby on the way.

On the first Saturday in February, about a week after the shower, I was in nesting mode. I felt an urgency to get the nursery done and put every gift in its place. Since Eric was busy working extra hours, I called a couple of friends from church to come and help me put the bedding in the crib, stock the diapers, and put the final touches on Arianna's new room.

They arrived to find me collapsed in the rocking chair, already exhausted. "You just rest," Cheryl said. "Jessica and I will finish this up. That's what we're here for. Tell us where you want this stuff, and we'll put it away for you."

We finished just as the sun was setting, and I thanked both of them before they headed home.

I met Eric for a date night dinner before the baby arrived. After eating and dreaming together about how our baby would look and how life would be, I shared with Eric the dream I'd had about our little girl.

"I dreamed that she had dark curly hair, and she looked like an angel. I kept watching her sleep peacefully, wrapped in a white blanket. She had a glow around her, and I kept saying, *Isabella, Isabella.* And then I woke up."

"Hmmm, it's pretty wild that she had dark hair. Isabella, huh?"

"Yeah, I know. I've always pictured her blond too. I looked up the meaning of *Isabella*: 'dedicated to God.' I like that meaning. But I like *Arianna* too. It means 'devout or devoted.'"

"I like *Arianna*. Why don't we keep it and make *Isabella* her middle name?"

"That's pretty. Arianna Isabella Joob. Devoted and dedicated to God."

We made our way home, and I collapsed into bed. I slept soundly until about one in the morning, when I was awakened by a gush of water.

I shot up in bed.

"Oh my gosh, Eric, wake up! I think my water just broke. We need to call the doctor."

We grabbed the prepacked suitcase on the way out the door. I tried to remember my Lamaze breathing techniques as we barreled down the expressway toward Lutheran General Hospital. When we arrived, we learned that my doctor was out of town. I would be guided through my first birth by a doctor I'd never met, who happened to be on call.

I was experiencing major contractions, and the hospital staff reassured me I would soon be given drugs to combat the pain. When a nurse came to check me again to see how far I'd dilated, she frowned. "That's interesting."

"What's wrong?"

"Well, I reached in to feel the head, and instead I got kicked. This baby may have turned around. I think you're breach."

"Oh my gosh. Now what?"

"Let me go talk to the doctor. If you're breach, the baby's feet are down, and you will need to have a C-section."

And with that she headed out the door.

To this point, everyone had been reassuring me I was in such great shape that this baby would just pop out without a problem. I wasn't prepared for a C-section.

The doctor checked me and confirmed the nurse's diagnosis. He walked me through the process. "We have a doctor who will be delivering your baby via C-section. She's delivering a set of twins right now, but you'll be up next. I see from your files that you're a model. I want to reassure you that we can give you the bikini-cut cesarean. Your cut will be very low, and no one will see the scar."

Right then, I didn't care about that. I just wanted my baby to be safe and healthy. I would do whatever it took.

After what seemed like an eternity, I was wheeled into the operating room. Eric had called his parents, my parents, and even Uncle Axel, who worked at the hospital. He reassured me that everyone at Christian Life Church would be praying, and that my parents' pastor in Minnesota was also praying. I was thankful to be having my baby on a Sunday morning!

As I waited alone for the anesthesiologist, fear came flooding in. I began to repeat the Scriptures I'd memorized during the pregnancy. *God has not given me a spirit of fear, but of power and of love and a sound mind.* . . . *Peace I leave you, my peace I give you. Not as the world gives, do I give to you.* . . . *Let not your heart be troubled, neither let it be afraid.*

God, please let everything be okay with my baby. Please let Arianna come out healthy and be 100 percent okay, and help me not to be afraid.

And then a major contraction nearly knocked me over. The anesthesiologist walked in at that moment.

"Well, that should be the last contraction you feel. I'm going to get you ready to have this baby. I understand you are a relative of Dr. Joob?" He had a warm smile. "We actually did our residency together. I could tell you some stories."

"Yes, he's my husband's uncle. So where did you do your residency?" I tried to get lost in the conversation with the anesthesiologist. It was better than thinking about what was happening on the other side of the curtain someone had put up in front of my face. I couldn't move my body, and I felt like I was being buried alive in cement.

Finally, the doctor asked me, "Do you want to take a look?"

Since my arms were strapped down, I couldn't move a thing. As they lowered the curtain, I saw Arianna being pulled feet first into the air, with her head hanging down. And then I saw someone dressed in blue surgical gear unwrapping a cord from around her neck. I didn't know if I should laugh or cry or scream. Eric was at my side, and I heard him whisper, "She just looked at me. She opened her eyes and looked right at me!"

When they got the cord untangled, they took her out of my view. I felt a slight panic. "Is she okay? Why don't I hear her crying?"

And then I heard the cry. *Thank you, God, for that beautiful cry!* My baby girl, Arianna Isabella Joob, was going to be okay.

God saw us through and protected her. The C-section was no mistake. I'm convinced that had I pushed her through the birth canal, the umbilical cord wrapped around her neck might have strangled her.

Now Arianna was fine, but I got completely sick. I held Arianna for a few minutes, and I was just beginning to breastfeed when nausea overtook me. I couldn't stop throwing up because of a horrible reaction to the morphine they had given me during surgery. Now I understood why they'd told me not to drink water while I was in labor. You never know if you may need surgery. *Lesson learned the hard way.*

I lay in bed, sick and miserable, and watched family come and go. I could barely hold or nurse Arianna. Eric tried to eat a giant sandwich in my room while he watched the Super Bowl, and it was more than I could take. I asked everyone to leave, and to take that sandwich out with them.

Thankfully, the reaction passed quickly, and the next day I felt somewhat normal again. I tried to hold Arianna as much as possible and to work on the breastfeeding, which wasn't easy to master.

We stayed in the hospital about five days, and then headed home to start our parenting journey. I felt sleep deprived but thankful to be home. The living room became my sanctuary since I couldn't walk up the stairs for a couple of weeks.

A few days later, Kelly called. "Are you up for visitors? Nick and I would love to come meet Arianna."

I quickly said yes. I welcomed anyone who wanted to visit those first few weeks. It was challenging to be stuck in the house, unable to drive myself around.

That late afternoon, the doorbell rang, and my friends arrived with bright eyes and faces radiating warmth and love.

Kelly was just two weeks from her own due date. We visited together in the living room, and Nick held Arianna. Kelly had a slight cold, so she decided not to hold Arianna that day. But just seeing my baby made her more than ready to have her own baby to hold.

They didn't stay long. And they'd barely driven a mile from our townhouse when Kelly's water broke, and she went into labor. Nick took her straight to the hospital, and she gave birth to Peter Zachary that night. We all laugh and agree that seeing me with baby Arianna triggered her labor.

Kelly and I remained close during those early days of being new moms. We visited often while breastfeeding our babies. As they got older, we took them on adventures together. God knew what I needed, and He was faithful to provide friends for every step of the journey.

Chapter 27

Undercover Angels

He shall give His angels charge over you, to keep you in all your ways.
PSALM 91:11

It was exciting to be a mom and to see Arianna hit milestones like her first birthday. We threw her a great Hello Kitty party at church. Her first trip to the emergency room via ambulance due to croup wasn't as much fun, but then there were her first steps at thirteen months. I was grateful to be home and not traveling so I could experience it all with her.

However, I still needed to work. I wasn't on contract with an automaker at the time, but my auto show agent helped me land a job at the Chicago Auto Show the February that Arianna turned one. My mom drove in from Minnesota to watch Arianna since I would work ten days straight, ten to twelve hours a day, and Eric was still busy working his jobs and going to school.

I was grateful to have family who could help, and the paycheck would make it worthwhile. My job was in a convention center ballroom, where we had presentations on a new truck. I oversaw the gift table, where attendees spun a wheel to win a prize. The week started off well. An onstage narrator did presentations on the truck several times a day, and after the presentation was over, visitors made their way to my table to play the game before they exited the ballroom.

About halfway through the week, I noticed that a man was repeatedly coming to our presentation. Each time he would come to my table. It was often dark in the ballroom, like a movie theater. Even when they turned up the house lights, it was still hard to see clearly.

Then things got creepy. The man began coming up before or after everyone else, so we were relatively alone. Most of my fellow workers were on stage or behind the scenes. The man would look me in the eyes and then, with a weird smirk on his face, he would pull out a handkerchief and put it over everything he touched. He wanted to repeatedly play the wheel-spinning game.

"Sir, I'm sorry. I can only give out one prize per day, per person."

He nodded and grunted, but he just kept staring at me in the same unsettling way. He never said anything to me. *Is this man mentally ill?* He wore the same clothes every day, and his pants were two inches too short. And yet he was a good-looking man. He reminded me of the actor Victor Garber.

He continued to come to my table, day after day, and it wore on me. I spoke firmly but kindly to him, and when that didn't work, I tried to ignore him. I wasn't sure how to handle the situation.

On the last Friday of the show, I got to McCormick Place early, which was my normal routine. I waited in the lobby near the ballroom, eating my breakfast and talking to Eric on the phone. I'd just hung up when an eerie feeling came over me. Something didn't feel right. I looked up from where I was standing, and just above me, on the other side of a railing stood the strange man.

"Good morning," he said in a creepy voice.

Oh my gosh. How long has he been there? Is it not enough to bother me all day, every day at the gift table? Now he corners me first thing in the morning too? I knew it wasn't my imagination. This guy was following me.

I told my supervisor about the man that morning, but I wasn't met with much sympathy. In fact, he basically told me to take care of it myself. Then I called my agent, and I didn't get much further.

"Just tell the guy to get the heck out of there and leave you alone!"

"I've tried everything I can think of. It would be one thing if I were on the main show floor, standing with a team of people in the bright lights. But I'm down in this dark ballroom by myself, and once the presenter leaves the stage, no other talent is in this room. I'm alone at the gift table, and I'm not supposed to leave my post. This guy waits for everyone to leave, and then he comes around and gets creepy."

"Okay, I'll let security know. But I think you just need to be firmer with him."

I ended the conversation feeling even more frustrated. My concerns hadn't been validated by those I was working with, so I figured I had to find my own way to stay safe during the last two days of the show. I even contemplated quitting. I was honestly afraid.

Finally, I decided to talk to my friend Marty, who is the McCormick Place concierge. He called a couple of his buddies who worked as undercover security for the convention center. Two older men in plain clothes showed up within thirty minutes, and thankfully, they took me seriously.

"We've got the description of the man you're talking about. And you said he's coming in here six to eight times a day?"

"Yes." I explained again what was happening.

"We know exactly who you're talking about. This same guy's going into the main halls and doing the same thing to a couple of the other girls up there. He keeps coming around repeatedly throughout the day, like he's stalking you. We'll have eyes on all three of you, and we'll station one of our uniformed security guards right here next to you so you don't need to be alone. We also suggest you have someone walk you to your car each night."

"Thank you for believing me and supporting me," I said, through the tears that were welling up in my eyes. "I really appreciate your help."

"No problem. That's what we're here for."

I felt relieved to be getting help and validation. Before the uniformed security officer came in, I made friends with a tall, friendly electrician who happened to be working in the ballroom.

"Whenever that guy comes around, you just come and knock on this door," he told me. "I'll come out and stand with you until he leaves. When the security shows up, they can help you from there." I did just that, and the electrician followed through.

When I got home from work that night, my mom was waiting up for me.

"How did your day go?" she asked. "I woke up this morning and felt led to pray for your safety. Did everything go okay?"

"Well, it's interesting that you ask. I'm thankful that you prayed. Let me tell you about my day . . ."

For those final two days, I felt much safer with the security guard next to me, the two undercover guys (who were actually Chicago police officers) checking on me periodically, and Marty stationed at his concierge desk not too far way. I thank God for all the people He sent to watch my back!

It reminded me of the verse I prayed over our family each morning from Isaiah 54:17: "No weapon formed against you shall prosper and every tongue which rises against you in judgment you shall condemn. This is the heritage of the servants of the Lord, and their righteousness is from Me, says the Lord." God kept His promise and His hand of protection over me again during the Chicago Auto Show that year.

Chapter 28

Manna from Heaven

*God's work, done in God's way
will never lack God's provision.*
HUDSON TAYLOR

March rolled around, and so did the spring bridal market. I worked again at the Merchandise Mart, but this time for a new client. I'd followed my contact at Symphony Bridal to a new company where she'd landed a job.

I was asked to be the lead model, which meant I would help find other models, train the newbies, and act as the liaison between the client and the models. My contact and I worked together to make calls and coordinate the models' schedules. It was time consuming, yet I was glad to work with friends and people I knew.

On the first day, I got there early. I made sure each person felt comfortable and took time to teach the new girls how to stand, walk, and pose on the runway in the various wedding dresses. We all worked a long day and modeled a lot of dresses at a number of shows.

At the end of the first day, one of the owners came back to our holding area. "Ladies, I just want to thank you so much for all your hard work today. You all have done an amazing job. In fact, this has been the best team of models we've ever worked with, and that's saying a lot. We've done shows in New York, Las Vegas, here in Chicago, and around the country. So thank you so much for all you've done for us here."

Wow! All our hard work had paid off, or so I thought.

We'd all verbally agreed to work for a four-day show, so it was an unpleasant surprise when my contact told us that models were not needed on the last day. We'd be paid for three days instead of four.

That was one of the challenges of the modeling business. Since we worked directly for the client at these shows, none of us had agents to back us up. And most clients at the bridal market didn't offer written contracts, so they could release models any time they wanted without paying them. I tried to stand up for the group since I was the lead, but the client didn't budge. There would be no extra money for us, even though they canceled less than twenty-four hours before the job.

"It's unfortunate they're canceling the last day," my contact told me, "but if you approach the owner with this issue, you'll be done. You'll never work for this company again."

"If this is how they treat their models, I don't want to work for them again."

On top of that disappointment, I'd been reassured that the client would "take care of me" for acting as the lead, assembling the team, and making phone calls. But at the end of the show, I only received a gift basket. I let my contact know that I'd expected to be paid something for my time, and eventually I did get a small sum of money. But in the end, we all received less than we'd expected.

It was a learning lesson all around for me. I eventually did write a letter to the owner to explain to her what happened, but I never got a response. When my contact called me that fall to work with that client again, I declined. I didn't want to work for people who didn't treat me fairly. In this business, sometimes I had to be my own agent and make decisions that protected me.

Thankfully that challenge was behind me, and the following weekend I flew down to Tampa, Florida, and into warmer weather. I was working a convenience store trade show for MET-Rx with a woman named Lucia, who lived in Florida.

It was a gorgeous, breezy, sunny day, and Lucia and I were chatting as we waited for the traffic light to turn so we could cross the street. We were catching up on life and family as we made our way into the crosswalk. I looked down and saw something glistening in the sun. It seemed to blow slowly toward me.

Are my eyes playing tricks on me, or is that a wad of cash in the middle of the street?

Sure enough, it was a pile of cash. There was no wallet or way to identify the owner. I snatched it up and turned to Lucia.

"Oh my gosh, look what I found! We need to find out who dropped it. Maybe I should holler to that group up ahead. I didn't see anyone drop it, but you never know."

Lucia shook her head. "No, don't say anything. They might just lie to you and say that it's their money so they can take it from you. I think that money is yours."

"Okay, if you think that's the right thing to do." I thought for a minute. "You know what? I think this is a gift from God. Last weekend I got shorted when I worked the bridal market. This helps make up for that loss."

The cash bundle contained almost two hundred dollars, and I felt so blessed and validated. I tried to split it with Lucia, but she wouldn't let me. Finally, I gave her fifty dollars, which she reluctantly took.

She wrote me a note later that week. "I just want you to know I took that fifty dollars and I donated it to our church. They're taking a special collection this week to help children in our community who can't afford to buy new shoes. I gave the money in your name."

It warmed my heart and nearly brought me to tears as I read her note. I always enjoyed working with Lucia, and we ended up having a successful show that weekend as we sold a record number of protein bars.

I learned a lot of selling techniques from Lucia. She trained me so well that I later went on to work trade shows by myself around the United States for MET-Rx. Lucia always showed support for my family too. She bought gifts for Arianna when she was born and helped me find some awesome giveaways, like stuffed animals and toys, from other trade show vendors to take home. God continued to take care of me, and He often worked through people at MET-Rx to bring encouragement and financial blessing.

Chapter 29

Small Potatoes

The secret of change is to focus all of your energy,
not on fighting the old but on building the new.
SOCRATES

About two weeks later, on an early spring day, my agent called. "Would you and Arianna be interested in shooting a commercial together? The client is looking for a mother and daughter. How old is your girl?"

"She's fifteen months now. This sounds like a fabulous opportunity!"

"Okay, perfect. She's in the right age range. Is she walking?"

"Yes, she is."

"Good to know. The client wants a child who can toddle along. I'm going to send you the details."

I looked forward to working with Arianna again (we had done a print job together when she was seven months old). The weather on our photo shoot date was warm and sunny, and everything seemed to fall into place perfectly, until the morning of the shoot.

When I changed Arianna's diaper, I realized all was not well. She had a loose stool and didn't seem quite herself. It was hard to know if it was a touch of the flu or if she was just teething. She wasn't running a fever. I called Paige, the agent, and let her know.

"Arianna seems a bit under the weather. It may just be teething, but she's a little fussier than normal." I described her symptoms to Paige.

"It doesn't sound like she's really sick, so if you're up to it, I think it's worth it to just go, unless she becomes a lot more ill in the next hour or so."

With Paige's approval, I said a prayer that Arianna would get better so we could make it smoothly through our first commercial together.

It was a bit stressful getting myself ready and Arianna and all her things packed and in place too. After loading the car with the stroller, diaper bag, and all things baby, not to mention all our clothing options, we were off. The location was on the north side of Chicago, where we would be filming in someone's house and neighborhood.

The crew welcomed us and helped me carry Arianna's things inside. We had a holding area in one of the bedrooms and space to hang our stuff. Arianna perked up as the morning went on, and I whispered a prayer of thanks.

We started by filming in the kitchen, and then we made our way to the sunshine outside. It was like a normal mother-daughter stroll as Arianna and I moseyed down the sidewalk. She was oblivious to the cameras, and I felt fulfilled being on set, enjoying my daughter, and making money at the same time.

After the commercial shoot wrapped, I called Paige to let her know things had gone smoothly after all. I told her I was open to doing more work with Arianna. I didn't realize it then, but things were shifting for me with work and family. This career certainly kept me on my toes.

A short time after the commercial shoot, I went for a run through our neighborhood. I like to combine my exercise time with prayer. Doing the commercial with Arianna had given me a desire to pursue acting and modeling again, but working for the John Robert Powers modeling school got in the way of scheduling auditions and shoots. The compensation there was modest. *God, should I stay at JRP and continue to speak/recruit, or should I take a leap of faith and pursue modeling again?*

As soon as I whispered that prayer, I saw a picture in my mind. In my hands, I held a number of small potatoes. There were so many they were overflowing, and there wasn't room for anything else. I felt God impress on my heart that if I continued to hold all those small potatoes, He could not bless me with the big potatoes He had for me.

God was nudging me to let JRP go and to step out in faith that He would bring bigger things.

I felt torn about leaving my position there. To me, JRP represented security. I was well liked, I enjoyed giving talks, and I was asked to return to the same schools repeatedly. I had a paycheck that I could count on each month. It was fulfilling to be with the tweens and teens. However, I sensed it was time for me to move on. Eric and I discussed my decision, and we agreed it was time for me to leave.

Less than a week later, I was at McCormick Place to work a medical trade show. Doctors and healthcare professionals come to these shows to earn their continuing education (CE) credits, and then they visit the show floor to check out the newest research and drugs. I worked for a pharmaceutical company as a booth facilitator. After the show ended the first day, I ran into my agent, Tamara, in the hallway.

"Hey, didn't you used to work for Porsche? I talked to Allie in Atlanta, and she told me you were on the team."

"Yes, that's right. I worked for Porsche for two years, and I worked with Allie. She's really sweet."

"Well, I'm in talks with Porsche right now, and I'm looking at taking over the account for the 2006–2007 season. Do you have a few minutes to talk with me about your experience?"

"Sure. This sounds like an exciting opportunity for you."

"And maybe you too," Tamara said with a gleam in her eye.

I told Tamara all the positives and negatives of my experience with the company. I filled her in on lots of details about Porsche Cars North America, and she shared with me where she was in the negotiating process. The conversation carried over to the phone, and Tamara told me that she would like to make me a team captain if she won the account. She planned to have two captains to oversee the team. Captains would go to all the major shows, where we would usually serve as the lead product specialists. We would also be sent to certain events and shows alone if Porsche needed only one representative. Tamara told me that she would let me know as soon as she received word from Porsche.

I can't believe Porsche could be in my future again. Is this why God urged me to step away from JRP? Are these the big potatoes? Can I handle being away from Eric and Arianna for up to two weeks at a time? I had a lot of questions, and I decided to commit the whole matter to prayer.

Chapter 30

Talks Too Much

In all realms of life it takes courage to stretch your limits,
express your power, and fulfill your potential.
SUZE ORMAN

Around the same time I began talks with Tamara about a possible return to the Porsche team, I was planning a trip to North Carolina to attend the She Speaks Conference put on by Lysa TerKeurst and Proverbs 31 Ministries. The preceding March, I'd attended a Hearts at Home conference with the moms' group at my church.

After one of her talks in March, Lysa had addressed the audience: "I'm wondering if some of you feel called to speak or write. If you feel that leading from God, I have a great way for you to pursue that calling at the She Speaks Conference this summer. If you are interested, please come visit me at the table during a break later today."

It felt like God was speaking directly to me through Lysa. Her words were like an arrow that hit the bullseye of my spirit. *I have to talk to her and find out about that conference. I think I'm supposed to go!*

I met Lysa and she told me all about it—and I couldn't get it off my mind. I thought about it constantly.

I gushed as I told Eric, "I think this is the next step God has for me. I can get the right tools to start my speaking career."

"It sounds good, but how much does it cost?"

"Well, somewhere between eight hundred and a thousand dollars."

"That's a lot of money. Have you thought of raising support like missionaries do?"

I thought of all the people Eric and I had helped over the years. Eric's words echoed in my mind. *If He wants you to go, He will provide the money.*

As I prayed, I felt prompted to ask certain people for help. I didn't want to argue with God, but some of the people He placed on my heart, I second-guessed. In particular, I really questioned when He impressed on me to ask a certain family member.

No way! He won't want to give me money to go to a speaking conference. And yet God kept nudging me to ask him. And so I finally found the courage to approach my brother-in-law, Alex.

"Sure, I can support you," he said, to my surprise. "How much do you need?"

I told him the amount, which was several hundred dollars.

"No problem. I've got you covered."

I was blown away. *I never need to doubt God's promptings again.*

And so in June, I was off to North Carolina for the conference. I flew to the conference a day late because I had already agreed to work a trade show. It had turned out to be a tough event. Then my plane was stranded on the runway in Charlotte until two in the morning. I didn't arrive at my hotel until around three.

It was not an ideal start to the weekend.

Nevertheless, my alarm went off four hours later at seven, and I got up to prepare for a long day at the conference. I was to meet my small group, which was led by Lysa TerKeurst herself, and then I would give the first of my prepared talks.

The ladies I met that morning at breakfast were fabulous. They encouraged me as I prepared to speak. I came dressed the part in a white two-piece skirt suit with a chartreuse camisole underneath.

I looked the part on the outside, but I was crumbling on the inside.

When it was my turn, emotions overwhelmed me. The late night on the runway, the crazy day I'd had at work, the lack of sleep, missing the first day of the conference, and stepping out into something as big as this were more than I could handle in that moment.

I opened my mouth to speak, and instead I broke down crying. While I tried to compose myself, the ladies around the conference table smiled and shouted affirmations to me.

"You've got this, Amy. It's okay—we all cried up there yesterday. We understand. We want to hear you speak. You are a beautiful woman of God."

Thank you, God, for their kind words and understanding. They reinflated my balloon, and I pulled myself together. As I started again, I whispered a prayer for grace. God showed up, and I made it to the end successfully. I had another opportunity to share later that day, and over the course of the weekend I got a lot of positive feedback and pointers on how to improve my speaking. I gleaned a wealth of information from the other keynote speakers and workshop presenters, and I even left the conference with a new friend and prayer partner.

Even so, I couldn't shake the disappointment that I had blown a big opportunity right in front of Lysa TerKeurst.

But during our private talk that weekend, Lysa said one thing that stuck like glue in the recesses of my mind. "You know, if you want to be accepted as a credible speaker, you need to write and publish a book." She looked at me with serious I'm-a-mom-and-I'm-not-joking eyes.

I gulped. "Okay. I've thought about writing someday, but it seems like a big undertaking. You've given me a lot to think about. Thanks for the advice."

As I flew home from North Carolina, I prayed about starting a speaking ministry. *Is it time now, God? Should I put together the bio sheet like they taught me and start reaching out to contacts? Do I really need to write a book first?* I waited to hear answers. I didn't know if it was time yet to launch a ministry, but I did feel like I was on the right track.

Back at home, I decided to continue honing my speaking skills. I reached out to Monster.com, a popular job-hunting website, and applied to be a speaker for their program "Making High School Count." I was accepted and invited to fly to Indianapolis for an intensive weekend of training. Prior to arriving, I had to memorize a fourteen-page script.

I spent many afternoons and evenings in our garage in the weeks prior to the training. While Arianna napped, I used that space like it was a stage. I was determined to land a spot on their speaking team.

I was nervous but prepared when I walked into the hotel that weekend. Part of me wished I was with my family instead of all these serious-looking strangers. Eric and Arianna were in Michigan, relaxing at camp and blueberry picking with Oma and Opa.

Michigan with my family seems a lot better than spending a weekend inside a hotel trying to perfect this long speech! Yet I knew I was being faithful to use the gifts God had given me. I still had a passion for youth and thought this would be a great way to motivate them to do well in school and go on to college—and at the same time, become a better speaker myself.

For three days, I went from one workshop to another. The first one was on voice projection. *No problem here. All the years of yelling at my four brothers and being on the cheerleading squad had prepared me for this.*

The next session focused on using inflection and animation in our voices. The following session was my favorite, as we focused on the content of our speech, the accuracy, and how to pace ourselves to finish in the proper amount of time.

When it was my turn to actually give the speech, I could feel my heart beating loudly in my chest. *You are not going to mess this up like you did at She Speaks. No crying. You're going to nail it, Amy.*

I opened my mouth, and the words flowed out. I felt confident, I shared boldly, and I remembered all the key points. All the effort I'd put into preparing paid off, and my speech came out sounding effortless. I felt God's hand on me as He gave me the words to speak and the ability to bring across the message clearly. I felt His presence, and I knew I was in my sweet spot, using the gift He gave me.

At the end, one of the judges remarked, "Wow, that was amazing. That's one of the best presentations I've heard today. I'm not sure what your future holds or if you will be on our team, but I know whatever you do in the realm of speaking, you'll be a great success."

"Thank you so much. I appreciate your encouragement." As I sat down, I whispered a prayer of thanks. Yes, my hard work had paid off, but ultimately, I had to credit God with my success.

I made the team. Now I could go into schools and give my speech to teens and hopefully motivate them to do their best, get good grades, and stay involved in activities so they could get into good colleges when they graduated.

I came home from Indianapolis feeling like I'd climbed a mountain and was looking out over a new horizon of opportunities. *Maybe I'm going to start my speaking career now!*

And then I got a call from Tamara that changed the direction of my life and career yet again.

"I have exciting news for you! I won the account. Are you ready to interview with Porsche?"

"Congrats, that's awesome news! Sure, tell me more."

"Like I said, I'd like to make you a team captain, along with Jen. We'd look to build the team around you two. But first you need to meet with Trevor. He's the new hire in marketing for Porsche Cars North America, and he'll manage the auto show circuit and other events."

"So Megan is gone?"

"Yes, she moved on. She and her husband opened up a dealership in South Carolina."

That was a disappointment. I'd liked Megan. "That's good to know. So I need to sell myself all over again?"

Tamara laughed. "Basically, but I've already filled them in about you. You just need to be yourself and let them know all the wonderful knowledge you already have about Porsche, and how you were a lead for them before."

"Sounds good to me!"

Eric and I did a lot of talking and praying before that interview. I was concerned about leaving Arianna for long periods, as she was just eighteen months old. Yet the money and benefits of the position would be great for my family. I also had a good rapport with Tamara and enjoyed representing the company.

"Remember the analogy you had about letting go of small potatoes?" Eric said. "I think this is it. This is God's plan. You took a step of faith and left JRP, and now you're being offered a much better opportunity."

"You're right. And I love to travel. I just don't want to leave you and Arianna for weeks at a time." I thought about my options. "And what about my speaking? I committed to Monster.com."

"The speaking is a great opportunity, but you don't know how much work they'll give you, and it doesn't pay as well as Porsche."

"Yeah. Let's pray God opens the right door for me."

We agreed to trust and put it all into God's hands. He knew best. If the door opened and I was offered a contract at Porsche, I knew I would be able to handle the travel and the intensity of the job. And if the door closed, then God had something better for me. It gave me peace as I eagerly awaited my interview.

Chapter 31

On the Road Again

Life begins at the end of your comfort zone.
NEALE WALSH

I sat across the table from Trevor and Tamara in the dimly lit restaurant at the O'Hare Hilton. I wore my black business suit and felt like I was at the starting line of a triathlon as I prepared to sell myself and gain back my old job.

Trevor leaned over the table and looked me in the eye as he spoke. "I know you worked for Porsche Cars North America from 2002–2004, and you were a lead product specialist for us in 2003–2004. Can you tell me some of your greatest challenges and your greatest highlights during that time?"

I took a sip of my water and swallowed slowly, stalling for time to think. I whispered a quick prayer that I would answer in a clear, concise way and say what Trevor wanted to hear from me.

"Well, I can start with the challenges. I think keeping both yourself and your team motivated during the long hours on the floor can be a challenge, especially at the big shows. I had an interesting time in Chicago in 2004 when a flu epidemic spread throughout the team on the final weekend. We all pulled together, worked some double shifts, and enlisted the help of a Porsche Club of America volunteer and even my husband. It all worked out okay in the end. I also survived a riot in Detroit the year before, but that's a whole other story."

"It sure does sound like you've had some challenging auto shows. And how about some of the successes you've seen?"

"I think one show in particular stands out to me. The Los Angeles Auto Show in 2003. It's over Thanksgiving, and we were there for a full twelve days. I remember we had very little dealership support as far as salespeople present, and we had a very large booth to cover. As you probably know, Porsche has a ballroom there, and the booth is set up like a museum. We had vintage Porsches and even the Carrera GT there. The girls rallied together to cover that much space, and thankfully we had full-time security watching over the Carrera GT. We also had help from one of the instructors from the Porsche Sport Driving School. He was amazing at fielding all kinds of questions. I think we collected a record number of leads at that show."

Most of the time local Porsche dealerships supported the auto shows by sending their salespeople to work shifts. Some areas of the country were better at supporting the shows than others. I think most salespeople would rather be at their dealership selling cars than at the auto show just talking about them. After all, they work on commission.

However, product specialists relied on good dealers who could follow up after the show with interested parties. We knew a lot about the vehicles, but we couldn't actually sell one to a serious customer. Having dealers there also helped us field the questions we got, especially at busy times on the weekends. And personally, I felt safer having some men in the booth. It made for a well-balanced team.

"I actually heard about that show," Trevor said. "You did collect a record number of leads, and I heard how hard you all worked. Southern California is one of our largest markets, and we appreciate the excellent job you did there."

We wrapped up the interview fairly quickly. As I walked out of the hotel, I had a chance to reflect. *I hope I land this job. I want to set an example for my daughter about what she can do. God, this one is in Your hands. I trust You with the outcome.*

A short time later I received the call from Tamara. The job was mine. The money was better than I'd hoped for. Jen and I were named team captains, and training was just a couple of weeks later. It was very clear to me and Eric that God had indeed orchestrated my move back to Porsche. We were even able to work out an agreement that he and Arianna could fly out and stay with me for a couple of days during the longer shows.

As soon as I finished my new training, I boarded a plane to Miami. My first event would be the relaunch of the 911 Targa, which was making its way back into the Porsche collection. To say I was nervous would be an understatement. As soon as I'd heard I would be working the event, I'd started studying all things Targa.

I got out my notecards on the plane and continued memorizing facts about the current Targa, as well as the previous generation. I knew that southern Florida was another of Porsche's largest markets, and I expected to meet many owners and enthusiasts at the reception.

God, I need Your help here. I'm a small-town girl, and I'm going to be rubbing elbows with high society. I don't want to mess up in front of these people or Trevor or the CEO. Thank You for giving me wisdom and confidence.

After finishing that prayer, I struck up a conversation with the person next to me on the plane. She was part of an excited, energy-filled group of young people seated all around me. My neighbor explained, "We're going on a mission trip together down to Honduras."

"That's so exciting. I've been on a couple of mission trips."

"That's cool. We've been planning this and saving for a long time."

"I did that too. Hey, do you want me to pray for you and your group?"

"Sure, that would be great. We'll take all the prayer we can get."

That prayer time on the plane turned my attention away from my own worries and cares. It was a welcome relief from the pressure I felt building.

When we landed, I met Stephanie, another Porsche product specialist from Atlanta. We checked into our hotel and got ready for the event.

We didn't need to think about what to wear. Each of us had three designer, custom-tailored suits and a variety of blouses and accessories to complement the uniforms. For every Porsche event, we were given instructions of what to wear, right down to our earrings. At home, I also had a casual wardrobe that included Porsche polos and khakis for summer events and races.

When we were ready, Stephanie and I hopped into a cab and made our way to the art museum where the reception was being held. Porsche was doing more special events like this to reach their target market, those people with the means to buy a Porsche. At normal auto shows, we talked to the general public, including people of all stages, ages, and socio-economic backgrounds. At auto shows, I talked to enthusiasts, tire kickers, techies, families, owners, and a handful of serious buyers. Most of the attendees at tonight's event, though, already owned Porsches, and so were more likely to purchase the Targa.

When the cab pulled up, Stephanie and I exchanged nervous glances. "Here we go," I said. "I'm praying that this is a success and we both know our stuff tonight."

"Me too."

The event wouldn't start for a couple of hours. I felt like we were entering the set of *Miami Vice*. Palm trees flanked the building, and beautiful people milled about, preparing. The parking lot was already full of 911s, Boxsters, and Caymans.

Stephanie and I checked in with Trevor, then made our way up to the rooftop, where the main party would take place. I would be stationed next to the new Targa, which was displayed in the middle of the outdoor party area.

"Wow, Trevor. How did you get this Targa up four flights of stairs?"

He laughed. "You ladies missed all the excitement. We brought the car up here via crane from the parking lot, and it was quite the harrowing experience. I think it took a couple of years off my life."

We laughed, and then Stephanie went off to her station downstairs by another Targa on the second floor. Later, she would assist Peter Schwarzenbauer, the CEO, in handing out some awards.

I began to relax as I took in the tropical surroundings. A balmy breeze floated through as guests arrived, dressed to the nines. Women in vibrant, flowing dresses mixed with men in sports coats and bright ties. They filled the rooftop, sipping on tropical drinks provided by models in long red dresses with red flowers tucked behind their ears.

I found my spot by the Targa and tucked my notecards into my pocket. My job was to share the facts and indirectly sell the vehicle. There was an air of warmth and hospitality in this group, and I decided I would just be myself and tell people what I knew about Targa and Porsche as a whole. I welcomed guests when they walked over to me and shared the facts about the Targa: the price, horsepower, engine specifications, safety features, and the like.

I noticed quickly, though, that this was a relational group. They didn't just want to know about the vehicle. They wanted to talk to me about my own life and my experiences.

In particular, I spoke with one couple at great length. At the end of the conversation, the woman caught me off guard. "We've enjoyed talking with you this evening. You're very knowledgeable, and you're a very kind person. Would you and your husband like to come down here for a holiday sometime? We would love to take you out on our yacht."

She handed me her business card, which included her phone number. *Wow. Are people this kind, or is it the wine talking?*

"Thank you so much," I stammered. "That's so generous of you. I can let my husband know. I appreciate the invite."

"Sure, no problem, darling. Seriously, call me anytime, really."

As we chatted, a light rain started falling. No one seemed fazed by the weather, so I stayed in my position and kept showing people the Targa and answering their questions. Eventually the light drizzle turned into real rain, and then a downpour. We all ran for cover under the awnings.

As we waited out the storm, I looked over the side of the building and saw a sea of Porsches in the lot. Other than the Rennsport Reunion, which is an annual celebration of Porsche Motorsports that showcases Porsche race cars from past and present, it was the most Porsches I had ever seen in one place at one time. I smiled as I took in all the impeccably dressed, warm, prosperous people.

The people of Miami left an indelible impression on me that night. They won my heart. I enjoyed the variety of people, their language, and their culture. I welcomed the adventure and where this new season would take me.

Chapter 32

The Eye of the Tiger

*So we shall let the reader answer this question for himself: who
is the happier man, he who has braved the storm of life and lived
or he who has stayed securely on shore and merely existed?*
HUNTER S. THOMPSON

In the fall of 2006, adventurous jobs were certainly not in short supply. Not only did I start traveling again with Porsche, but I also received a call to work the International Manufacturing and Technology Show. I should have known it wasn't going to be a normal job based on one of the first phone calls I had with my agent.

"We're going to need your measurements. The client is having dresses made for you by a seamstress up in Wisconsin. I'm going to email you a list of everything she's looking for, and then you need to call her with those measurements."

"Okay, this is interesting." I was often given a shirt to wear for trade show work, or a dress or fitness clothing were given to us, but I'd never had a dress made for me. "What will we be doing?"

"Well, I know you'll be wearing tiger print. You're working for Walter, a well-known company up in Milwaukee. They seem very professional."

"Tiger-print dresses? What type of company is this?"

"Don't worry," my agent said. "I've worked with this client before, and they're completely reputable. They want the measurement for two inches above your knee, so they won't be sleazy."

"All right, time will tell. Six days in a tiger-print dress. I'll let you know how it goes!"

There can be many surprises in this business, and this job did not disappoint. I arrived the first day at the Lakeside Center at McCormick Place decked out in full tiger stripes from head to toe. Thankfully, the dresses were comfortable and classy, despite the pattern.

I made my way to the designated meeting place outside the hall, where our contact from Walter introduced herself.

"You ladies know you will be working with live tigers during the show, right?"

I swallowed hard. *Did she just say live tigers? Did I hear her right?*

I saw the other girls nodding, and someone shouted, "Yes! This is going to be amazing!"

All I could think about was how Steve Irwin, the Crocodile Hunter, had died days before, while filming *The Ocean's Deadliest.*

If the professionals can't do this and live, what chance do we novices have against wild beasts?

I lingered there a moment, feeling small and vulnerable. I wasn't as bold as the stripes on my dress, but I finally pulled together all my courage and decided to press forward.

Move over, Vegas, here comes Chicago!

We made our way to the Walter booth, and there, right in the middle, loomed a large, black, iron, circular cage, like one you might see in a three-ring circus. There was a waist-high fence about two feet from the cage to keep the audience far enough back.

We were informed that two tigers would be wheeled in from the loading dock right before each show. One of their trainers would join them in the cage and have them eat meat off a stick for the crowd.

The trainers and tigers came from Hollywood. They had a holding area on the loading dock in a converted elephant trailer they'd driven in from the West Coast earlier that week.

When we met the lead trainer, he told us, "Ladies, what I'm going to need you to do is play 'Vanna,' if you will. You will assist me in opening the curtain around the cage right before the show. We will run six shows each day."

"Okay," I interrupted. "I'm just wondering . . . if we're inside the fence to reach the curtain, can the tigers reach through and touch us?" As the lead on the show, I felt not only responsible for myself, but for the other models too.

"Well, technically yes. Their reach is almost to the fence. So if you ladies can stay as close to that fence as possible while you open the curtain, that would be great."

I swallowed hard again. *Is this some kind of practical joke? Are we being punk'd? Is someone going to jump out and let me know this is all a big setup?*

Or maybe not. This was real. All I could imagine was a big tiger paw reaching out to shred my legs.

As I pondered this information, I slowly paced around the booth with a forced smile on my face. I prayed. Then we were called over again.

"All right, ladies, we have a new plan. One of the trainers will open the curtain inside the fence. You can stand outside the fence and help with crowd control. These animals are professionals, and they've done many commercials and movies, but they are still wild animals. They can innately sense weakness. If they see someone elderly, handicapped, or even a small child, they will tend to zero in on them. We need you to just stand between the tiger and that person if you notice that happen."

Tiger security. I needed to add that one to my resume. *I will now commence a 24/7 prayer vigil.*

Then I noticed the top of the cage was completely open. When I saw one of the trainers alone, I decided to ask a few more investigative questions.

"So let me ask you, can these tigers jump out of there?"

He looked at the cage. "Well, they could jump out of this, but not in one jump. They'd have to climb the side of the cage to get out. Honestly, we've never done a show like this before, at least not quite like this. The cage is smaller than we requested, and this is not exactly the setup we were expecting. And really, we thought PETA would come in right away and shut us down. But that hasn't happened yet. If we were in California, we wouldn't make it to the first show."

"Okay, this is a bit disconcerting, and yet somewhat exciting. I will be praying for you and everyone in the booth the entire day. Thank you for being honest with me so I know what I'm getting into here."

As they say in the business, the show must go on! When the trainers brought the tigers out for the first time, my heart rate escalated. I watched in amazement as two stately creatures sauntered into the cage and sat on their designated chairs. The trainer remained calm as he held up the stick with the meat. The tigers sat up and lifted their front legs into the air as they reached for the treat.

They were indeed beautiful. And huge. I found out later that they were Siberian tigers, which can span eleven feet. I didn't want to see them face-to-face without that cage between us. And I swear the animals looked at us models especially carefully since we were wearing tiger print.

I couldn't wait to tell Eric about my day. "This job is a real beast . . . literally! You're not going to believe what we are doing!"

After I explained it, he reassured me. "You'll be fine. If they jump out, you can outrun them. You just ran a marathon last year."

"I ran for endurance, not a sprint. Do you realize tigers can run fifty miles per hour? This is completely nuts!"

"Well, you have a job to write home about, that's for sure."

"Please just pray I finish this job in one piece."

"You'll be fine. If you can't outrun them, you can outsmart them."

"Uh, you're the one with street smarts, remember?"

For six days, I did not relax. I literally prayed nonstop during every show. And then on day five, things got ugly. Something upset one of the tigers during a show, and it growled and attacked the other tiger. They got in a scuffle of sorts. I watched as the trainer slowly backed up and almost pressed his back against the iron bars of the cage. He was in the greatest jeopardy. I almost started praying out loud.

Maybe God has me here for such a time as this? So I can pray that nobody becomes tiger meat!

The scuffle slowly died down, and I exhaled. I'd been holding my breath. One of the trainers walked over and started talking to me. We all needed to decompress.

"I told them we need to get these tigers out and let them get some energy out. They have been cooped up in that trailer all week. I tried to get permission to let them walk around here after hours, but they wouldn't let us do it."

"Oh my gosh, that would be crazy! What if you lost one of them somewhere or they attacked some unsuspecting security guard? But I understand you're pushing their limits. Thankfully there's only one more day to go!"

I can't imagine a night security guard or custodian just faithfully doing their job and then looking up to see a tiger walking down the hall toward them.

Is this job for real, or is this all a dream?

Thanks to God, the job ended without incident. I sure hope Walter's Tiger Tech tool line received a boost in sales from that whole circus act. At least I didn't get bored during that show, as the tigers drew volumes of people to the booth. It was the most exhilarating, memorable job I have ever worked. And I'm thankful I survived to tell about it.

Chapter 33

Close Call

When you're traveling with someone else, you share each discovery, but when you are alone, you have to carry each experience with you like a secret, something you have to write on your heart, because there's no other way to preserve it.
SHAUNA NIEQUIST

Blustery cold rolled in. Winters in the Midwest can be manageable at best and brutal at worst. This one was moving slowly. It was another dreary, frigid January, and I was heading back to Detroit for the North American International Auto Show. I tried to psyche myself up for the nearly three weeks I would spend there. I hoped and prayed that this time around, things would go more smoothly. I couldn't imagine weathering another riot.

This year, the Porsche team was booked at a hotel in Greektown, one of the more upscale, developed parts of downtown Detroit. I was rooming with Nikki, who was the lead product specialist for this particular show. Since the hotel was set up like a suite, Nikki took the bedroom and I took the pull-out couch in the living room so we could each have separate quarters. We both had TVs, and the bathroom was between the rooms, so the arrangement seemed perfect.

The first day of press week, I joined the other product specialists as we marched into Cobo Hall wearing our red winter trench coats. We wore identical designer suits in blacks and grays with matching scarves and jewelry, and we made quite the statement during our grand entrance.

The team was ethnically diverse and filled with women who excelled in modeling, acting, dancing, narrating, journalism, business, and more. Porsche only hired college graduates, and I felt proud to be with such well-rounded women and thankful I had made the cut this second time around.

At the booth, we got situated in our locker room. We always had locker space to store our belongings and a break room with tables and chairs that doubled as an office. The team could get important work done and also have a quiet place to enjoy our lunch and dinner breaks. Leads could work on post event show reports and others could study scripts for upcoming jobs or work toward their master's degree. We were well taken care of during the shows.

We were preparing for Porsche's big press conference. All the executives from Germany had come in again. I had seen them at all the major shows year after year.

One of them pulled me aside. "It's good to see you again, Amy. I know you've worked a number of shows over the years. Thank you for the excellent job you are doing for us here in the United States."

I made my way to the other side of the booth, walking a little taller and a little lighter with each step. Later I headed to our break room and dialed Eric's number.

"Hey, you are not going to believe this." I told him about the compliment I had just received.

"That's cool. I'm in Springfield, backstage right now. Everything is set up, and we're ready to go."

He was there with our brother-in-law, Alex, whose lighting company was doing the production for the inauguration of the new governor of Illinois, Rod Blagojevich.

"Sweet. We're about to start our press conference."

"We're about to start too. It's amazing we're both on big jobs at the same time."

We hung up and got back to work. I headed over to my designated spot, thinking about my family. Oma and Opa took care of Arianna when both Eric and I were out of town, which wasn't often. Usually Eric took care of her, and friends from church babysat while he was at work. Dale and MaryLou were like extra grandmas, and Amber and Laura were friends from my moms' group who had young children too.

After my long days at the Detroit show, I was thankful to head back to the hotel and crash for the night. Usually I worked either 10:00 a.m. to 6:00 p.m. or 2:00 to 10:00 p.m. On bigger shows, I would occasionally work from noon to 8:00 p.m. We needed the most coverage in the evenings, because that's when it was busiest with the after-work crowd. If it was a weekend or a holiday, the floor was crowded all day and night.

About halfway through the show, Eric and Arianna drove in to see me. Arianna was a month shy of two years old at that point, and I always cherished their visits. We booked a hotel together in Dearborn, near the Ford Museum. While I worked, they did some sightseeing.

One morning as I was getting ready for work near the bathroom, Arianna was around the corner near the bed. It was quiet, and then suddenly I heard this heavy breathing. It sounded like a very small, female version of Darth Vader breathing through his helmet.

What the heck is going on in there?

I walked into the other room, and Arianna smiled at me with her mouth half open.

"Arianna, what are you doing there, sweetie? What do you have in your mouth?"

I could see she had something, but she was determined not to spit it out. I looked closer and realized she had gotten into my Altoids. She had two of the small, powerful white mints on her tongue, and she was fighting the intensity. *This is pretty impressive. She has a lot of sisu, just like her mama.*

Our strong little girl had a teddy bear backpack with a tail that doubled as a leash, so that Eric and I could keep track of her in large crowds. She wanted to run everywhere, and I didn't want our beautiful, towheaded toddler getting lost in Detroit.

Their short visit gave me a renewed energy to finish the auto show strong. By the end of the show, though, I was more than ready to go home. To stay energized, I worked out daily, read my Bible, prayed, and worked on the scrapbook I'd been making for Arianna.

I was sitting in my room one night, working on the album, when suddenly I heard a booming voice coming from the hall.

"Open up! I know you're in there."

The owner of the booming bass voice was standing right outside my room, pounding on the neighbor's hotel door. His voice became more persistent. Somehow he managed to enter the room and a major scuffle ensued.

Every hair stood up on the back of my neck, and I nearly froze in fear. When I finally mustered up an ounce of courage, I jumped up, grabbed my phone, and ran into Nikki's room. I hurled myself into the air, cleared all the steps and then did a somersault before landing face down on the ground. I lay there, shaking, next to the bed.

Nikki was watching television when she saw me dive onto the carpet, and she broke out into loud belly laughter.

"What is wrong with you? What are you doing?"

"Don't you hear that? Something's going down next door, and it sounds like someone might have a gun. I don't want to get shot. I have a husband and a two-year-old daughter to go home to."

The scuffle reached a crescendo of yelling, swearing, screaming, and furniture rearranging. It seemed to escalate with each passing second.

"Yeah, I can hear that, but I'm not worried. That kind of stuff happens in my neighborhood all the time. We'll be fine."

"It might be common for you, but I'm not used to it. I'm staying down here until that stuff dies down. Do you think we should call the front desk?"

Nikki shrugged. "They haven't given us very good customer service so far, so I'm not sure they'd do anything. They might not even believe us."

"You're probably right. This is nuts. I'm going to pray."

"Sounds good to me. I'm going to finish watching my show." Nikki's voice trailed off as she relaxed on her bed. The argument next door didn't faze her, but I decided I would stay in my posture of prayer until it was over. I felt safer on the floor. *If God can't show up and bring a peaceful end to this, I'm not sure who can.*

Thoughts swirled around in my head as I lay there. *Maybe I can't call the front desk or 911, but I can call on God.* I thought of God's phone number, Jeremiah 33:3. "Call to Me, and I will answer you, and show you great and mighty things." I cried out to Him silently. *God, please bring this thing to an end and get me out of here alive. I just want to go home and see Eric and Arianna. I pray that no one shoots a gun or hurts anyone in this place. In Jesus's name.*

Finally, I heard more voices in the room next door, and then things gradually quieted down. The whole episode seemed to go on for hours, but I'm sure it only lasted a few minutes.

The next day our friend, the Rev, drove us to work in the hotel van. Rev was a young African American who worked at the hotel part time and pastored a church part time. He had a love for God and for people, and it showed. It seemed as though he was our Porsche angel on that trip.

"Here's the skinny on what went down last night," he told us. "It turns out you had a big-time drug dealer staying next door to you for close to two weeks. Apparently, he was dealing right out of his room, and he had different women coming and going. Last night his girlfriend found out where he was and brought some of her friends over to confront him and the women he had in there."

"That explains the guy with the big voice. What happened then?"

"Well, someone called the front desk. Security and even the police showed up to break up the whole scene. You should have seen those women in there. They kept talking crazy to the police. Like 'you can't make me leave here. And don't tell me what to do!' Those women were crazy, and that guy is in a heap of trouble."

"I'm so thankful he's gone. What a relief! I know God protected us, Rev. I was lying face down on our floor, praying. I was freaked."

He chuckled. "We serve a good God, and I'm thankful He was watching out for you two. He always hears and answers our prayers."

A minute later, I said, "That explains why I kept smelling pot in the bathroom! It must have been coming through the vent from next door. I'm so glad we are safe now."

And with that, Rev dropped us off in front of Cobo Hall, so we could start our next shift at work.

Never a dull moment here in Detroit. I'm thankful God has my back all the time.

Later that week, I had another opportunity to exercise my faith muscles. I walked into the convention center bathroom and heard a woman crying hysterically. She was in one of the last stalls with the door open. A friend was trying to console her. They appeared to be employees of Cobo Hall, as they had on matching work shirts.

"Excuse me, is everything all right? Is there something I can do to help you?"

The friend responded, "No, she's fine. We don't need any help. But thank you for asking."

"Okay. Do you mind if I pray for your friend?"

"Sure, go ahead."

The woman seemed to be in a whole lot of emotional pain and perhaps physical pain, too, so I prayed for comfort and healing. I prayed God would intervene and make Himself real to her in that moment. I never learned what she was going through, but it seemed deep and heavy.

I always prayed for "God opportunities" as I worked. I didn't want to just earn a paycheck. I wanted to do something significant. I wanted to make a positive difference on every job in every city. It made the sacrifice of being away from home more meaningful.

Chapter 34

Hope in Houston

Your best days are still out in front of you.
JOEL OSTEEN

I flew home from Detroit and had one day off before I was
scheduled to leave for Houston, Texas, and the auto show there. I used
the downtime to take Arianna for her first haircut. It was important for me
to be there for major milestones like this in her life.

I was working a lot at this point; in a forty-five-day period, I had worked
forty-three days across three auto shows and a print job. To help me keep
my sanity, Oma and Opa brought Arianna to Houston for a couple of days
so I could see my girl. I know it was God's grace that kept me during that
time, because I never got sick. In Houston, I was working with a product
specialist named Danette, a friend who always encouraged me to think
and share only positive thoughts. One Sunday, she and I decided to go to
Lakewood Church and see the famous pastor, Joel Osteen. In the South,

auto shows don't start until noon on Sundays, so that gave us time to go to church.

Danette and I took a cab to the former Compaq Center stadium, where the church meets. We were dropped off at the front door, and I noticed there were very few people around. Perhaps this wasn't the main entrance that regular attendees used, I thought, and that's how they know if someone is a visitor. I figured there must be a huge parking garage somewhere to accommodate all those people.

An friendly man greeted us at the front door. "Ladies, it's a pleasure to have you join us here at Lakewood today. Where are y'all from?"

"We're from Chicago. We're here working the auto show and have the morning off, so we decided to come to church."

"That's wonderful! You look lovely in your matching suits. If it's okay, I'm going to take you down to the front of our church. We save our very best seats for our visitors each week."

"Thank you so much," Danette chimed in. "I watch Joel a lot on TV because we travel so much. It's great to actually be here in person."

The man smiled. "If you're interested, following the service I would be more than happy to take you to meet Joel and Victoria in person. Would you like to do that?"

Danette and I looked at each other with wide eyes and smiled. "Sure, that would be great!"

As we talked, the man led us up to the front of the church and showed us open seats in the front row, right in the middle. I was in awe.

"I feel like one of the pastors on staff here, sitting up so close," I said. Seconds later, the worship band started to play, and a worship leader took center stage.

I leaned over to Danette. "I think that's the best greeting and welcome I've ever received at a church. No wonder this place is filled to capacity."

The sermon Joel preached that morning was both encouraging and timely. He talked about how God uses current circumstances in our lives to prepare us for our calling and what He has for us. Joel spurred us on, as he said that nothing is ever wasted with God; He will work all things together for good.

Following the benediction and an invitation to come forward for prayer, the same greeter came back again.

"Ladies, how did you enjoy the service?"

"It was amazing. Really uplifting."

The greeter led us up some stairs to a designated spot in the lobby. We waited in a line with about thirty or forty other people to meet the Osteens. We thanked our guide, and he left to assist others.

When our turn came, Joel and Victoria smiled and extended their hands for warm handshakes.

Joel spoke first. "Welcome to Lakewood, ladies. So where are you visiting from this morning?"

"We're from Chicago." Danette responded with a smile.

"Wonderful, and what brings you down here to Houston?" Victoria asked.

I explained that we worked for Porsche and were here for the auto show.

"Oh my goodness," said Victoria. "Joel used to drive a Porsche when I first met him."

"Ah, I see you have great taste," I said.

Danette and I explained how we watched him on television when we traveled for work. I added that I'd like to speak and even write a book one day.

"That's wonderful," he affirmed. "I believe that you can do that if you keep that vision central in your mind and keep speaking His word until you see that dream come to pass. Do something each day that brings you closer. God will make it happen!"

We thanked them for their time and headed to the front door, where we'd arranged for the hotel shuttle to pick us up. We already had our work clothes on, so we went straight to the convention center.

I couldn't wait until lunch to call Eric. I told him about meeting the Osteens, and then told him what was on my heart.

"What if you and I start fasting and praying together one day a week? I read that fasting, praying, and giving are key to seeing God move in your life in big ways. It's like Matthew 6:33 says, 'Seek first the kingdom of God and His righteousness, and all things will be added to you.'"

And with that, Eric and I started a new practice that kept us bonded together and invited God to intervene in our lives in a more powerful way.

The Houston show wrapped up on Super Bowl weekend, and the Chicago Bears lost to the Indiana Colts. As I walked into the hotel lobby after my last day of work, I saw a man standing not far away. He was wearing a New Orleans Saints T-shirt, and I noticed his head hung low and his shoulders slumped.

I heard that still, small voice. *Go over and talk to him. See if you can pray for him.*

I walked over and glimpsed the musician Prince on TV, performing the half-time show. "Hi, I see you're wearing a Saints shirt. Have you been to New Orleans?"

"Yes, ma'am. I'm from there. I lost everything during Hurricane Katrina, and I've been here ever since. I've been trying to figure out how to make it since then."

"I'm so sorry to hear that. I've been to New Orleans a few times. I can't imagine what you're going through. Do you mind if I say a prayer for you?"

"Sure, that would be great."

And with that, I prayed the words God put on my heart to pray. I wished I could do more for the man. I told him about Lakewood Church and after I asked him his name, I told him I would be praying for him the rest of that week.

Overall, the time in Houston was uplifting. I felt relieved that the show had been slow and manageable, since Danette and I were heading to the Chicago show next. We would need all the strength and stamina we could muster.

Chapter 35

Trouble in Paradise

*I am not the same having seen the moon shine
on the other side of the world.*
MARY ANNE RADMACHER

After working the Dallas Auto Show in early March, I had a day off to see my daughter, repack, and get ready to leave for Hawaii for a week. I was honored to represent Porsche there, but it hurt to be away from Arianna so much. I often woke in the middle of the night with a heavy heart. I just ached to see her. I fought tears as I prayed God would give me the strength to continue working.

This time around was especially bittersweet. Arianna would stay in Illinois with Oma and Opa, and Eric would join me for the Honolulu Auto Show near Waikiki Beach. It would be the first time either of us had been to Hawaii.

As Eric's dad drove us to the airport, I looked in my wallet and had a startling surprise.

"Oh my gosh, I don't have my license! How am I going to get on the plane?" There wasn't time to turn around and go all the way back before my flight took off.

"Why don't you call the airline and ask them what you can do?" Eric's dad suggested.

"Ugh! Of all the times to forget my license . . ." I trailed off as I dialed the number for the airline. When someone answered, I told them my predicament.

"Well," the customer service agent seemed to think out loud. "Do you have any other picture IDs in your wallet? If not a passport, maybe a state ID or a Sam's or Costco card?"

"Yes, I have my Costco card! There's a picture on the back."

"Okay, that should work. I'll put a note in here that you don't have your license. Is there anyway someone can send it to you before your return flight?"

I looked sheepishly at Eric. "Well, my husband's going to fly out to Hawaii to meet me a little later. He may be able to run home and get it for me."

"That would be helpful," the agent responded. I hung up and told Eric and his dad the good news.

"Where do you think you left your license?" Eric asked. "You had it in Dallas to board the plane there, right?"

I tried to picture the last few days. "Yes, I remember showing my license when I went through security, and then I slipped it into my boarding pass envelope, and I put that inside my purse. Then last night, I cleaned out my purse. I threw that old boarding pass away . . . um, I think you'll find my license in the upstairs bathroom garbage."

"So now I need to go all the way back to Huntley to fish your license out of the garbage?" The volume and pitch in Eric's voice rose higher with each word.

"Ahh, yes that's what I'm saying. Remember you married me for better or worse? At least we're still going to Hawaii!"

The stress over the lost driver's license melted away as we arrived in paradise. Both Eric and I made our flights on time, and I waited for him about an hour at the airport as my flight arrived first. Then, when we checked into the Hilton Hawaiian Village and Beach Resort and mentioned my agent's AAA status, we discovered we were eligible for a room upgrade. They moved us to the luxury towers, with a private pool, complimentary breakfast, and drinks and appetizers in the evening.

Our first job was to find a dry cleaner for my auto show wardrobe. The hotel prices seemed too expensive, so we put all the suits, blouses, and scarves in a couple of backpacks and went for a jog around Waikiki, looking for a less expensive place. I felt like we were contestants on *The Amazing Race*, running through unfamiliar territory and trying to beat the clock, since it was nearly five o'clock and we thought the cleaners would close soon.

Finally, we found a dry cleaner about six blocks from our hotel and arranged for twenty-four-hour service. Then we asked some locals for sightseeing suggestions. Everyone kept mentioning the Polynesian Cultural Center, so we followed their advice and spent an entire day there, learning about Hawaiian customs and practices. We even went to an authentic luau.

Hawaii was captivating, and I could barely get a wink of sleep. The ocean view from our room was majestic, with turquoise water and white sand that seemed to stretch on forever. Palm trees swayed softly in the breeze. Lovers walked hand in hand along the beach, the women in flowing dresses with colorful hibiscuses tucked behind their ears. The gentle sound of the waves and the beauty of the sunset over the water made me want to sit and relax on the beach all day.

Instead, I went to work. On the second day of the show, I walked to the hotel during my dinner break to join Eric for appetizers and drinks.

The hotel had fresh veggies and dips out, and the bartender offered to make drinks of our choice. I opted for a nonalcoholic piña colada since I had to go back to work for another four hours.

Eric and I relaxed on a private balcony that overlooked the ocean and enjoyed our time together. I finished my veggies and most of my drink. As I went back to the show, I was feeling really full, but by the time I got to the booth, I realized my stomach didn't feel right. I had severe pains in my abdomen, and a tidal wave of nausea came out of a seemingly calm ocean and overtook me.

I had to run for the bathroom. It was a small show, so I was working alone at the booth, but I quickly asked my new friends at Jaguar and Mercedes to keep an eye on things.

I got to the stall just in time. I vomited repeatedly, which left me feverish and dizzy. I had one of the worst stomachaches of my life. I said a silent prayer for God to help me.

Within minutes, my friend from Mercedes came into the bathroom. "Are you okay in here?" she asked. "You didn't look so good, and you've been gone awhile."

"I'm so glad you're here," I panted. "I'm really sick. I think it must be food poisoning." The thought of food made me gag again.

"Okay, I'll go make sure your booth is covered. I'll put out more brochures for you. Take your time. Do you want me to call someone?"

"Thanks. Give me a minute. I may need to call the dealership. I'm scheduled until ten, but I don't think I can work right now."

"Good idea. I'm so sorry you are sick, especially when you're in Hawaii. Maybe if you get a good night's sleep you will feel better tomorrow?"

"I hope so," I responded weakly. "Thanks so much for checking on me." Thankfully the dealership was understanding when I called them. I assured them that I thought it was food poisoning, and that I planned to be there for my shift the following day.

I practically crawled back to my hotel and called Jeri, one of my prayer partners.

When I told her about my situation, she assured me, "I'll be praying for you, for sure. How's Eric? Is he feeling okay?"

"Yes, he's fine. I'm glad he's here. This is as sick as I've ever been."

"I'm glad he's with you."

I went straight to bed, but sleep did not come easy. I was in and out of the bathroom all night and lost track of how many times I threw up. I wasn't sure how I would work ten hours the next day.

In the morning Eric looked at me and said, "Hey, I brought some black dress clothes with me. Why don't I go to work with you today? You can sit at the table, and I'll stand and greet people and hand out brochures. You can answer questions if needed."

"That would be amazing. Thank you."

"Have you called to let your agent know what's going on?" he asked.

"No. I need to tell them that 'hula girl' has taken a hit but plans to work anyway."

"At least you're keeping a sense of humor. And you haven't thrown up for what, two hours now?"

"Yeah, but I think I'm going to live on soda crackers and 7-Up today."

Eric worked with me for the first half of my shift. Since it was a smaller show and a weekday, it wasn't very busy, and I felt a little bit better with each passing hour. By my dinner break I was ready to try some normal food. I was slowly on the road to recovery.

The rest of the show was a breeze. We were working in a picturesque place with floor-to-ceiling picture windows, so it didn't feel like work at all. The warmth of the sunshine streaming through the windows and the palm tree branches blowing gently in the wind soothed my soul.

Eric and I spent our final day together touring the island and climbing Diamond Head, which overlooked Waikiki Beach and most of Honolulu. Then the employees at the Porsche dealership gave us a tour and swag before driving us to the airport. We thoroughly enjoyed the majestic views and experience, but our lives were not complete without Arianna. We looked forward to going home and embracing our little girl once again.

Chapter 36

MET-Rx Marathon

All life demands struggle. Those who have everything given to them become lazy, selfish, and insensitive to the real values of life. The very striving and hard work that we so constantly try to avoid is the major building block in the person we are today.
POPE PAUL VI

When I returned from Hawaii, my work with MET-Rx picked up again. Lee and I flew to Columbus and braced ourselves for a long and busy weekend at the Arnold Classic, a premier professional bodybuilding, figure, and fitness competition. The event also included competitions in cheerleading, lacrosse, gymnastics, tae kwon do, fencing, swimming, and every other sport I could imagine. Kids and adults came from every state.

Lee and I were both a little worn out, as I'd been traveling, and Lee had been recovering from some health issues. We decided we would put up our feet as much as possible and relax when we weren't working.

Lee and I were there to promote the Karma energy bar from US Nutrition. We got to wear tasteful, comfortable yoga outfits. But the event was busy, and we were inundated with people all the time.

On the other side of our booth was the MET-Rx stage where they were holding competitions. Various hopefuls performed the snatch, clean and jerk, and other weightlifting exercises as they competed against one another. Jesse Marunde, a World's Strongest Man competitor, emceed the event.

The entire expo hall was filled to capacity. The aisles were crammed with attendees from every sport. Fitness competitors and bodybuilders walked next to cheerleaders and ultimate fighters. It was possibly the most fit, athletically diverse group of people I have ever seen.

People moved through the aisles much like partygoers move through the streets of the French Quarter during Mardi Gras. Swarms of athletes fought for samples of our Karma bars and other products. Lee and I could barely maneuver in our space behind the counter as people snatched samples and barraged us with questions. We couldn't keep up with the demand.

At one point, Lee looked at me and said, "We need to give each other some sanity breaks here. We can take turns going to the bathroom. It's going to take ten minutes just to walk the few feet there and another ten minutes to stand in line."

"I hear you. I've never been in such a crowded space. I'm trying not to have a panic attack, and I may need to go on an extra coffee run."

"Good idea. If you stand in that crazy line, it's my treat."

And so we adjusted and ended up having fun in Columbus. We caught a glimpse of Arnold Schwarzenegger, the founder of the Arnold Classic, in front of our booth. We also had some encouraging conversations with Jesse, who was training for the next World's Strongest Man contest. He was married and had a baby, and as serious as he was about his sport, I could see that he was first a family man and proud new dad.

By the time we reached the airport Sunday night, Lee and I could barely move. We collapsed into our seats at the gate and nearly fell asleep before our plane boarded for Chicago. "I'm so glad you were here with me this weekend," I told her. "I don't know if I could have done it without you."

She smiled. "I know it's hard, but I think you're doing the right thing right now. You're helping to support Eric as he finishes school, and he's almost done now. And you're making good money doing jobs you enjoy. God has opened up some amazing doors for you. He'll give you the strength to handle it all."

"Thanks, you always bring the right perspective, Lee. You are like the big sister I asked Santa for every year."

God knew when I needed a friend and extra support during those hectic times of back-to-back jobs. *This is just for a season, and you are helping Eric finish college. It will get easier from here. Your hard work will be rewarded.*

Chapter 37

Harrowing Flight

Safety is not the absence of danger, but the presence of God.
JEANETTE WINDLE

Not only did God bring me the support I needed, but He provided protection as well. With as many miles as I was flying every year, eventually I was bound to hit some bumpy air. And that's exactly what happened the following month when I was scheduled to work two convenience store shows in a row.

Lori called me and gave me the scoop on my travel arrangements. "I have you flying into Baltimore, and from there you'll take a smaller plane to Lancaster, Pennsylvania. That way you can fly out immediately to Des Moines in time for the next show. Are you okay flying in a smaller plane?"

"Sure. I flew in a helicopter when I did a short film here in Chicago, so a small plane shouldn't be a big deal."

"Great! How's Arianna doing these days?"

"She's getting into everything. Before one of my last trips, she got into my suitcase and wouldn't get out. She kept saying, 'Arianna go too!' I wish I could take her. She is so beautiful and sweet, and she loves books."

"I bet she's smart and beautiful, just like her mama."

And so I flew to Baltimore, where I had a short layover and grabbed a bite to eat. When I got to the gate for my connecting flight to Lancaster, I realized just how tiny the aircraft would be. There was only one other passenger boarding, and we had to walk down some stairs and out onto the tarmac.

The passenger, a young lady, reached for some Dramamine in her purse. I looked at the plane and asked her if she had any to spare. She obliged. I chewed that little pill quickly and whispered a prayer that I wouldn't get sick and that we would all make it safely to our destination.

As we approached the Cessna, the copilot motioned us over to the front of the plane. He opened the nose and loaded our suitcases inside. I kept my MET-Rx duffel bag with me, and I laughed with my fellow traveler as we tried to figure out how to board this puddle jumper. I was fit, active, and healthy, and yet I questioned whether I could cram myself into that small space.

Once on board, we met a handicapped woman who was already seated behind us. We buckled in, and the pilot announced we would take off shortly. I looked at my newfound friend with wide eyes and a half-smile and prayed again that we would make it safely to Lancaster.

The takeoff was stimulating. Since I was seated right behind the copilot, I could see and hear everything happening in the cockpit. In fact, I was so close that I could reach forward and grab the controls if I wanted to. The instrument panels were all in full view, and it seemed overwhelming. I watched in amazement as the flight crew maneuvered and worked various gauges, dials, and steering controls with ease.

Shortly after takeoff, we "came into some weather," as I heard the copilot mention to the pilot. It was completely disconcerting to look through the windshield of the airplane and see nothing but thick white fog that grew darker and darker. I couldn't fathom how the pilot knew we were heading in the right direction, or how he could maneuver the plane at that speed and elevation when he couldn't see where he was going. I just had to trust that he could see things clearly through his instruments and dials.

Then the turbulence came, and I've never experienced anything like it before. We not only bumped up and down, but we dropped. Significantly. And then we shook back and forth, like a swing gliding right and left. It seemed like the nose of the plane was constantly jerking sharply to the right or left. We were jostled in every direction, like items being tumbled around in a giant clothes dryer.

The woman next to me started to throw up in her "discomfort bag," and the lady behind me started moaning. I'm not sure if she was sick or scared or a combination of both. I gripped the copilot's seat in front of me for balance and tried not to alarm him as he adjusted the dials.

I started praying for the pilots and quoting Scriptures out loud. I'm sure no one could hear me over the noise of the engine and what seemed like a tornado we were attempting to fly through.

The two men piloting our aircraft remained remarkably calm through it all. They talked to air traffic control and I continued to talk to God, and somehow we made it through the turmoil. The dryer eventually stopped, and we landed safely, albeit bumpily, in Lancaster.

"Well," I heard the pilot say. "That was one of the most challenging flights I've had during my career."

When I finally exited the plane, I stumbled, off balance and a little nauseated. I felt like I'd just got off an intense roller coaster ride. I was more than thankful to be alive. I wanted to shout "Hallelujah!" I momentarily thought about kissing the ground, but that just made me feel queasier.

Instead, I called for a taxi and checked in with Eric while I waited. And then I noticed a text from my small group leader, Steph, at church. "God put you on my heart, and I felt led to pray for your safety. Did you land in Lancaster yet?" I blinked back tears as I read her text. God is so good! He is so faithful to protect us and watch over us no matter what we are going through. And He even prompts others to pray right when we need it most.

To say I felt an aversion to small aircraft at that point would be putting it lightly. I didn't look forward to flying back to Baltimore at the end of the show. I even contemplated renting a car and driving to Baltimore, but I knew that would make me miss my connecting flight, which would make me miss my next job, which would let down Lori and everyone else at MET-Rx.

I gave myself a little pep talk instead. *I've run marathons and triathlons, swam around an island, went to college across the nation where I knew no one, and I've given birth to a baby. How hard can this be? Get in that darned plane and fly back already!*

By the time I was scheduled to leave Lancaster, my equilibrium and emotions were returning to normal. Thankfully, there were blue skies and sunshine that day, and the flight back was smooth and uneventful. It made me realize that I shouldn't let one bad experience stop me from moving forward in life and enjoying all the wonderful opportunities God has in store.

Chapter 38

Too Much Time Away

'Tis one thing to be tempted, another thing to fall.
WILLIAM SHAKESPEARE

The summer of 2007 was packed with traveling for Porsche and MET-Rx, character jobs at corporate events, print jobs, and trade shows. The work continued to flood in, and I juggled as many jobs as possible into my overbooked schedule. I felt like a hamster on a wheel, and I couldn't slow down or get off.

At one point, I was home and sorting through the mail. I found a credit card statement for a card I didn't know we had. Angry, I immediately called Eric. "I'm holding a statement for a MasterCard. Can you tell me about this?"

"I was going to tell you. I got a card so I could get some things for our place. Nothing major. I bought Arianna some new stuff for her room."

I calmed down some but still felt upset. "Well, I wish you would talk to me first. I'm working hard, and I don't want to worry about extra bills."

"I know, but it's not easy. You're gone all the time, and I'm here at home juggling school, work, side jobs, and Arianna."

"I know. It's hard for me to be away from you guys too. And honestly, I've also been doing some stress shopping." I'd started living off half my per diem so I could shop with the other half.

"We just have to get through this for now. We'll take it day by day."

And so as the warm days of summer marched on, so did our busy lives. In early July, I flew out to work the American Le Mans Series races with Julia, another lead product specialist. I flew into Hartford, Connecticut, late that night from Chicago and waited for Julia to arrive from Orlando so we could drive together to our inn, which was an hour away. Her flight was delayed, and I worried as we still had to pick up the rental car.

I glanced at the clock in the airport. *12:55 a.m. Is the rental car place even open this late, and how are we going to get to work by 7:00 a.m.?*

Julia landed soon after, and we picked up our car and headed out around one thirty in the morning. Neither of us had realized before just how beautifully lush, yet extremely dark, it was in Connecticut. Huge trees with full branches loomed over us, and only a sliver of the moon shone through.

We followed our directions, but for some reason we couldn't find our inn that night. Julia kept driving down dark, winding roads while various wildlife popped out in front of our car. Those gigantic trees began to feel like they were closing in on us. We saw a closed gas station, and then we drove around some more and found that same gas station again. It was nearly three in the morning and we needed to be at work in four hours.

"I think we have a couple of options here," I said. "We can call my husband and see if he can give us directions, but we'd have to find a name for one of these roads to tell him where we are. Or we could call the police and see if they could come and lead us to the inn."

"Or we could just call the inn and tell them we're lost and see if someone there can give us directions," Julia pointed out.

"We're going to call this late?"

"Someone's going to have to wake up anyway when we check in."

And with that Julia called the inn. The owner answered on the first ring, which I thought was either a good sign or a spooky one. She gave us better directions, and we arrived a short time later to find an unkempt mansion that looked a hundred years old. It had a freaky vibe in the dark, and I thought it seemed haunted. From the moment I walked in, something didn't feel right.

The owner of the inn welcomed us. "I'm so sorry you had trouble finding the place. I keep getting after the county to put up a road sign at the intersection. The locals know where they're going, but visitors can never find the place."

"I'm just relieved we aren't driving in circles anymore," Julia said. "I was getting dizzy."

"Well, here's your key. Your room is on the top floor." She led us across the creaky floor to a narrow, slanted staircase. I followed Julia, whispering my concerns about the inn to her as we lugged our suitcases up the stairs. Of course, I never traveled light.

"I think this used to be a saloon or a brothel," I told her. "I feel like bad things happened here. I don't want to stay," I complained in a strained whisper.

"I don't want to be here either," Julia reassured me. "But it's three thirty in the morning, and we have to be at work in less than four hours."

"This is completely nuts. Why did we fly in so late? Do you feel like working a twelve-hour day on two hours of sleep?"

Julia put the skeleton key in our door and tried to figure out how to maneuver the antique knob. "Well, that's my fault. I had an acting job today, and I requested to fly out late. You could have flown in earlier, but then we would have had to rent two cars."

"Well, good to know. You owe me a coffee for this."

We tiptoed into the room, furnished with antique beds, dressers, and radiators.

"I'm going to lie down and catch a nap until five," Julia announced. "Then I'll get up and get ready."

"I'll get up right before you. I need a shower—" But even as I made this comment, I saw that Julia was already dozing off. Just a couple of hours later, we were back in our rental car, loading up on coffee and Red Bull at a gas station before we drove another hour to the racetrack in Lime Rock. Like many of the tracks Porsche sent us to, it was in the middle of nowhere. The countryside in Connecticut was absolutely stunning. Rolling hills, clusters of trees, and green as far as the eye could see.

We arrived in Lime Rock. As we entered the racetrack grounds, Julia said, "Let's not tell Trevor and Lee (Trevor's boss at Porsche) what time we got in last night. We don't want them to think we can't do our job well today."

"Yeah, you're right. Let's just hope this Red Bull works. And I think I'd rather sleep here tonight instead of back at that haunted inn."

"Come on, it's not that bad."

We found our spot at Porsche's VIP hospitality tent, which catered to owners attending the race. Porsche had two Le Mans Prototype 2 cars competing, with two drivers per car. The race would last three hours and was meant to test the endurance of both drivers and vehicles. The car that completed the most laps in that time would be the winner.

It was a gorgeous day, and our two Porsche teams were racing very well that season, which made our job more exciting. Julia and I worked the front desk of the air-conditioned tent, which housed a Porsche on display, tables and chairs covered in white linen, a big-screen TV, couches, a bar, and a buffet. Porsche served its guests gourmet food and drinks throughout the day, and the drivers and Porsche race team hosted press conferences and meet-and-greet times.

Our job was to greet and check in guests, answer questions, and help manage the flow. We made it through the day with the help of a positive atmosphere and a lot of Red Bull. As Julia and I drove back to the inn near dusk, we were met with a surprise. The country road we were on went right through a farm, and a herd of cows had gotten out of their pasture and were standing in the middle of the road. And they weren't moving.

It took almost an hour for those cows to cross the road. I offered to jump out and try to scare them, but Julia squashed the idea. If I ended up getting trampled, she reasoned, she wouldn't be able to drive me to the hospital quickly.

Whenever I traveled with Julia, I knew thrilling exploits were just around the corner. That made life on the road much more exciting.

Chapter 39

Life in the Fast Lane

The world asks, "What does a man own?"
Christ asks, "How does he use it?"
ANDREW MURRAY

In July, I got a very sad email from Teresa at MET-Rx. Jesse Marunde, the World's Strongest Man competitor Lee and I met at the Arnold Classic, had died. He was only twenty-seven years old, but he'd had a heart attack while training near his home in Washington. I was deeply saddened, remembering his magnetic personality and how much he'd loved his wife and new baby.

I thought about Jesse a lot that summer. I finally had some downtime, since there were no auto shows at that time of year, but I still worked events over long four-day weekends. I thought about how the traveling was affecting me, my marriage, and my family. Like Jesse, I wanted to live full throttle and accomplish my dreams, yet I wanted to be there for my family, too, and not lose them in the pursuit of everything else. Was I still on the path God had called me to be on, or was it time to start moving in a new direction?

During this time, I flew to Ohio with Jen, my fellow Porsche team captain, to work the races at Mid-Ohio. We would be in the Porsche hospitality tent near the racetrack for the American Le Mans Series races again, which happened the same weekend as the Indy Car races.

Jen and I arrived at our hotel to find that the arrangements were less than stellar. The registration desk in the office had bars in front of the window. The grounds were unkempt, and the rooms were musty smelling. The walls were banged up from partiers or lack of care, and there was an unsettling vibe about the place.

This wasn't the first time we'd found ourselves in less-than-desirable accommodations. Most of these racetracks were in the middle of nowhere, with very few hotels around.

On a positive note, I was with Jen, and she was a tall, strong, and intimidating woman. She actually stood two or three inches taller than me and carried herself with a presence. People knew Jen meant business, and they didn't want to mess with her. I really liked that about her, and together I felt like we were unstoppable. We could take on any roach, animal, or crazy person that came close to our hotel or Porsche display.

Midway through the first morning at the racetrack, a confident-looking man with a huge smile that lit up his face came into the tent while I stood at the welcome counter, ready to greet guests as they arrived. His presence and demeanor commanded my attention as he extended his hand to shake mine. I almost looked behind me to see if he was looking for someone else.

"Hi there," he said. "I'm Roger Penske, and I'm wondering if you've seen Jeff in the tent this morning?"

"Nice to meet you. I'm Amy Joob. And yes, I believe Jeff was here earlier, talking to Lee. Do you want me to get Lee and see if we can find out where he went?"

"Sure, that would be great."

Roger Penske was the crew chief for Porsche, which meant he was like the head coach or manager of the team. It was his job to direct the drivers and the crew during a race.

I walked into the management office and let Lee know that Roger was looking for him. The two of them carried on a short conversation, and then Roger walked toward the door. He turned before he left, waved, and smiled. "Thanks, Amy."

Talk about a great first impression. He's one of the most confident, polite, and humble men I've ever met. No wonder he's so successful.

We were preparing for a press conference in the tent. We had winning cars that season, and the excitement and momentum was building with each race.

The drivers came in one by one in their race gear. That year, our Porsche drivers hailed from Germany, France, and Australia. The drivers kept themselves lean and fit so they could handle the intensity, speed, and long stretches they spent in the race cars. I also heard they tried to weigh less so the car could go faster.

I often had the chance to talk to the drivers when they came in for these conferences and post-race parties. They seemed to enjoy talking to the team in the tent as much as we liked talking to them. At this particular race, a flirting rapport began to develop between me and a couple of the drivers. Jen and I took a picture with them, and one of the drivers commented, "Hey, are you going to hang that picture up in your house? Maybe in your room over your bed?"

I laughed, but I was serious when I said, "I don't think that would go over so well with my husband. He's German, too, and one German is all I can handle in this lifetime." I wanted the driver to understand I was married once, for life. "One and done" had been Eric's and my philosophy from the beginning.

When the drivers left, thoughts swirled around my mind. *Maybe I'm getting a little too close for comfort. I need to make sure my heart is in the right place. Eric and I have been apart a lot over these past couple of years, but he's the one I want to spend the rest of my life with.*

I knew what I needed to do. I found out where the racetrack's chapel was and when services would be held that weekend. I planned to go as soon as I could. In the meantime, I called Jeri, one of my accountability partners, and asked for prayer.

"I'm at the races at Mid-Ohio, and I feel like all these weekends away and missing church is starting to catch up to me. I'm getting too flirty with some of the drivers, and I want to make sure I do things right. Will you pray for me?"

Jeri prayed, and then I went to chapel during my break. I could only stay about thirty minutes, but it was enough time to get my heart right with God. I sang and listened closely to the message the chaplain gave. I was pleasantly surprised to see many people at the service that morning.

After I left, I felt refreshed and strengthened. I readjusted my perspective to remember that this was a job—my family was at home, and I was working hard to bless and help them. I needed to look to God for strength to do the work He called me to do, and I needed some good, quality time with my family soon.

The weekend ended up being a huge success. Some of the VIPs who were scheduled for rides on the racetrack didn't show up, so Trevor arranged for both Jen and I to go. I rode along with a female professional race car driver, and she was phenomenal. She took the curves and straightaways with grace, ease, and speed. The whole time she zipped around the track, shifted, and worked the clutch, she carried on a relaxed conversation with me. As I exited the race car, I felt proud to be a woman.

"I want to be like you when I grow up. And I'm not joking. Thanks so much for the amazing ride!"

"Anytime. You know where to find me," she responded with a warm smile.

Working for Porsche at the races made me think about becoming a professional race car driver myself. However, it's an expensive sport, and most drivers start as kids driving go-carts. *Well, a girl can always dream.* As memorable as that weekend was, I looked forward to embracing Eric and Arianna and enjoying every minute I had at home with them.

Chapter 40

Tested

God never uses anyone greatly until He tests them deeply.
A. W. TOZER

A couple of weeks later, in early August, I drove up to the quaint, picturesque town of Elkhart Lake, Wisconsin. Julia and I were scheduled to work together again, and this time our agent had rented a house for us because all the hotel rooms were sold out.

We met at the house and walked gingerly into the unfamiliar place. It felt a bit awkward, since people lived there all the time and had just vacated the premises so we could be there. Their personal belongings were there, and their fridge and cupboards were stocked with food. I felt a bit like Goldilocks roaming around the three bears' cottage.

Eventually, we got settled. We both opted for downstairs bedrooms. I picked a pink-themed girl's room filled with stuffed animals and horse figurines, and Julia picked a blue boy's room that had a sports motif.

We woke up early to make our seven o'clock call time at the track. We got fixed up, grabbed our breakfast, and hustled out the door of the garage to our car.

We worked a long twelve-hour day at the track and came home exhausted. That's when we realized that in our haste to leave that morning, we hadn't noticed that we'd locked the door from the garage into the house. We didn't have a key to the house, only the garage door opener.

Julia groaned. "Do you remember reading the instructions that said, 'Make sure you don't lock the inside door of the garage'?"

"Yes, I do, but I could swear this morning when I left, I checked to make sure it was unlocked."

We circled the house and tried every window and door, every nook and cranny. Nothing else was unlocked, nor would it budge.

We had a few less-than-desirable options. We could break down a door, enter through the chimney, or call the homeowner and tell them our predicament. We opted for the latter.

The homeowners were gracious. "Lucky for you, we decided not to drive to Minneapolis like we planned this weekend. Otherwise, we would be a six-hour drive away."

They came right away and let us back in. We made sure we knew how to work that inside door, and we even thought of propping it open the next day.

As we finally sauntered into our rented house, I suddenly realized that it was the last day I could take the monthly Porsche test. Things had been gaining speed as the summer wore on, and I'd totally dropped the ball on this. Now I had just four hours before the deadline.

"Oh snap," I told Julia. "I didn't take the monthly test yet. Did you?"

"Yes, ma'am. I sure did." Still, Julia hopped onto the family's computer in the den and pounded on keys. Finally, she turned around looking half irritated and half dejected.

"No cigar. I can't figure out their password. You're out of luck here, my friend."

Neither Julia nor I had laptops, and this was before smartphones made it easy to access anything online.

"Well, I could call Eric, and he could read me the questions over the phone and I could tell him the answers."

It wasn't ideal, but it's what I did. Eric logged into my account and walked through the test, question by question. I finished around ten that night. It seemed pretty humorous at the time to listen to Eric ask me questions about makes, models, engines, pistons, and drivetrains. But in hindsight, it would have been smarter to just take the test late and accept my penalty, if there was one. But I wanted to please everyone at Porsche and at my agency, because I really wanted to do a good job and keep working with them all. Oh, the paralyzing fear that paints the canvas of a perfectionist.

I was feeling increasing pressure to not just keep up with work expectations, but to do an excellent job. The pressure of juggling my various jobs and my personal life were at times colliding like two racing vehicles at an intersection. I needed to decide whether I would pursue the career path or scale back and focus on my family.

At the track in Elkhart Lake, I talked with Trevor.

"How do you do it?" he asked me. "How can you be on the road this much when you have a husband and a little girl at home? How old is she now?"

"Arianna's two and a half now. It's not easy, and sometimes I don't know how I do it. I have an understanding spouse, and we're both determined to see him finish school, so I just keep working hard. And I pray a lot."

"Well, you do a great job, and you sure know these cars. We appreciate having you on the team."

Our race cars kept coming in first and second, and it was exhilarating to ride the high of Porsche victory after Porsche victory. It made the pull to stay in the job even stronger.

I had a lot of time to think as I drove through the countryside of Wisconsin on my way home from that event. The scenery reminded me of Minnesota, and that got me thinking even more about my family. My questions turned into prayers as I drove over the border into Illinois. *God, please show me what You want me to do. Make my path clear. Please keep our family together.*

Chapter 41

Rewarded

Be patient. The best things happen unexpectedly.
WWW.LIVELIFEHAPPY.COM

The weather was humid and sweltering in Chicago in August of 2007. My slowest months were generally July, August, and January, so I felt relieved when any work opportunities came my way. I was grateful when my agent told me she had a booking for me in the Hamptons off Long Island, New York.

I would be working solo as the only Porsche product specialist at the Hampton Classic, a weeklong equestrian competition and a swanky affair. Porsche was one of the main sponsors.

I flew into a small airport in Islip, New York. Coincidentally, that's the headquarters for US Nutrition (now called The Nature's Bounty Co.). It seemed like my work worlds were melding together. I picked up my rental car, an electric blue Dodge Charger, and felt a mixture of enthusiasm and trepidation as I started my journey east. There were no hotel rooms available in Southampton that night, so I needed to spend the first night in a motel about an hour from the airport. A fellow passenger on the plane had told me that the location wasn't the safest area on Long Island.

I don't remember the name of the town where I stayed, which is just as well. The entire experience was a nightmare. I pulled up to a rundown, dilapidated motel in a wooded area. I saw a rusty, broken, dangling motel sign and a dirty pool with green algae growing on the bottom. Beat up, nasty pool furniture was tossed around inside and out of the pool. I couldn't even find the motel office.

An eerie feeling hung over me like a heavy fog. With every fiber of my being, I wanted to turn around and drive as far away from that place as possible. Instead, I paused and prayed. *Lord Jesus, please keep me safe here, and if there's any possibility that I can stay somewhere else, please open up another motel room somewhere!*

As I parked, I noticed garbage strewn around and a few motel guests sitting outside of their rooms, grilling and drinking. The people looked rough around the edges, and they talked loudly while smoking cigarettes. I reluctantly checked into my room, dropped off my suitcase, and promptly left the premises.

It was late Saturday, so I didn't call my agent. Instead, I called Eric. "I'm here, and it looks like the Bates Motel. I think it's the creepiest place I've ever seen. I don't want to stay here by myself."

"Yeah, I looked it up online, and it got really bad reviews. I didn't want to scare you."

"I wish you would have told me. Maybe I could have found a different place."

"Well, it's only for one night, and the next place is supposed to be amazing. It got excellent reviews."

"Great. Please pray for my safety tonight. I'm going to drive around and see if I can find another motel with a vacancy."

"Do that," Eric encouraged me. "We can pay for it. It's no big deal. I'd rather have you stay somewhere safe and comfortable."

"Thanks. How's it going on your end?"

"Good, everything's fine. I'm getting ready for the Tums job at Latino Fest. Matt from church is going to be my interpreter."

Eric had been a DJ for a number of years, ever since he was in junior high. His hobby turned into a side job, and now he did paying gigs like wedding receptions, corporate parties, birthday and holiday parties, and outdoor events like Latino Fest, which was held in Grant Park in Chicago. As the DJ, Eric used his charismatic personality to get the whole crowd dancing. Matt, who was preparing to be a missionary in Mexico and spoke fluent Spanish, would help him communicate with the partygoers. It was a win-win for everyone.

I spent a couple of hours scouring every motel and hotel in the area before I came to the painful conclusion that everything was sold out. Stock car races were going on nearby, and all lodging was full to capacity. In my agent and Porsche's defense, I booked the job only a couple of weeks earlier, and by that time most hotels were already sold out.

I stopped at a strip mall, where I ate dinner and tried to distract myself in a bookstore. I called Jeri and asked her to pray, which made me feel a little bit better. Then I reluctantly drove back to hunker down for the night.

And hunker down I did. I pulled my Charger into the parking space in front of my room. The car had tinted black windows, and the electric blue paint was in mint condition. The rims were shiny, and I realized that this car may be my saving grace. Perhaps my ride would make me look like a drug dealer, or at least like I fit in here. Maybe no one would mess with me.

I hesitantly walked back into my room, which had windows on both the west and east walls. There was even a window in the bathroom. I shut every drape, put a towel over the bathroom window, and barricaded myself in. I put the table, chairs, and my suitcase against the door.

I prayed over the room. I got out my Bible and read it aloud. I wanted God's presence to fill that room. I slept with one eye open and my Bible and cell phone on my chest. I think I got an hour or two of sleep at most, but I woke up without a scratch or a bug bite. I took a record-breaking fast shower in the outdated, semi-clean bathroom and left at 5:30, relieved to see the motel in my rear view mirror. I felt like I could breathe again. I stopped for coffee and started to relax as I drove toward the venue, still an hour away. The farther I drove east, the more beautiful the scenery became. Even the atmosphere changed, and the heaviness I'd felt back at the motel lifted.

When I arrived at the Hampton Classic, I realized that my journey was symbolic of life. Sometimes we have to go through a lot of crap before we make it to the promised land. It's never fun when we're going through it, but when we arrive on the mountaintop, it sure is worth it.

I arrived a little early due to my eagerness to leave the motel and found myself in a location that was the complete opposite of the night before. The land was lush, and the setting was immaculate. I parked in a grassy field and took a moment to thank God for keeping me safe.

I met my contact for the event, Michelle, a short time later, and she walked with me to the Porsche tent which showcased three of our vehicles. It was one of several pristine, white tents that surrounded the main area where the horse-jumping competition would take place.

I felt like I was in a dream. There was more wealth, luxury, and prominence here than I had ever seen. I could see the stately, spacious stone mansions that lined the white sands of the Atlantic Ocean. Small airplanes and helicopters routinely flew by. Lush green grass mowed in neat diagonal patterns carpeted lawns that were framed by blooming flower gardens and bushes. The luxury vehicles lining the driveways were the type only seen in the movies.

Since I'd grown up in a humble small town, the contrast was staggering. Yet I reminded myself that I was there to represent the Porsche brand and I had the knowledge to talk to the many serious buyers who would be there.

That evening, I drove to a beautiful red-brick bed and breakfast. I parked my Charger next to several Porsches, BMWs, Maseratis, and Lamborghinis. I gulped and prayed that I wouldn't back into any of those vehicles in that cozy parking lot the next morning.

After a warm welcome, a quiet night, and a hearty breakfast, I made my way back to the venue the next day. I knew I would be working alone for the first few days, and on the weekend someone would come from Porsche Cars North America to help me. The owner of the local Porsche dealership let me know someone from his establishment would come out periodically to detail the cars.

The morning started off slowly, and I enjoyed people watching and soaking in the sunshine and ocean breeze. As I stood there smiling, I noticed a gorgeous woman approaching with some teenage boys and small dogs. It was Christie Brinkley! She smiled and warmly said hello as she passed me on her way toward the main tent.

Ironically, the week before I left for the Hamptons, I'd stopped at Walmart to get some last-minute supplies for my trip. The friendly greeter there had said, "You sure are pretty. You look just like Christie Brinkley." Although I couldn't agree with him, the compliment gave me a boost of confidence, and here I was, less than a week later, saying hello to her. *God does work in mysterious ways!*

One afternoon during the middle of the week, a striking man made his way into the tent. I thought he looked familiar, but I couldn't think of who he was. And then it came to me. It was the actor Billy Baldwin.

My heart beat a little faster, but I tried to calm myself and smile. *Just be yourself, Amy. Act normal. You can do this.*

Billy smiled at me and then stopped, stood back, and took in the GT3. "What's the price tag on this?"

I explained the price and different specs of the GT3, and he seemed genuinely interested in the car. "How can I get my hands on one of these?" he asked.

I handed him a card. "Here's the information for the nearest dealer. I'm sure they will be able to help you." My heart was beating out of my chest as he had such confidence, presence, and swagger.

He thanked me and left to join his family in the food tent. I let out a deep sigh and prayed God would give me strength to just be myself and do my job well, no matter who I ended up talking to that week. It seemed like He was trying to stretch me and teach me confidence as I rubbed elbows with high society.

Later that day, one of the event officials came over to the tent. "Who's taking care of the two vehicles stationed out by the entrance off the dirt road?"

I explained that someone from the local dealership was coming out and taking care of those cars.

The man rolled his eyes. "Well, no one has touched those cars in the last day or two, and they look horrible. They're covered in dirt from all the cars that drive by."

"I'm sorry to hear that," I told him. "I'll let the dealership know right away and find someone to take care of it. Thanks for telling me."

The dealership sent someone that day to detail the cars, but the next morning I checked those two Porsches before I got to work, and I saw they were covered in dust and dirt again.

Even though it wasn't officially my job, I decided those filthy vehicles were not a good reflection on Porsche. I might as well suck it up and wash them myself. Eric had done some side work as a car detailer, and he taught me all the tricks of the trade, so I knew what to do.

I found buckets, a hose, and towels, and every morning I washed the cars. *This isn't my job, but I will do it, and I believe You will bless me for it.* It reminded me of the verses in Colossians 3:23–24, "And whatever you do, do it heartily as to the Lord and not to men, knowing that from the Lord you will receive the reward of the inheritance; for you serve the Lord Christ."

It was extremely humid in the Hamptons in August, and washing cars was a sweaty job. I'd have to go to the air-conditioned bathroom each time after to freshen up before I started my day in the tent.

On the final day of the Classic, I drove the now-familiar route to the event feeling homesick. I got teary-eyed as I prayed over the event, and for Arianna and Eric back home. I thanked God for the opportunity to work in such a fascinating place, that I overcame another bout of food poisoning earlier that week, and that I would get to see my family the next day.

I cleaned the cars first, and then I prepared the tent for the final day. Heather, the representative from Porsche Cars North America, approached me. "You've done an excellent job working here this past week, and I want you to join us in the main tent today. Feel free to eat and drink whatever you want, and you can watch the competition with us too."

I was blown away. This type of thing rarely happened. But around lunchtime, Heather found me, and we all made our way into the tent. This was where all the VIP attendees gathered to watch the competitions; it had a full view of the arena. The finals of the equestrian jumping event were underway, and the main tent was full of people. I stood back and admired the white linens and fresh flowers on the tables scattered around where guests could eat.

I felt like I was on set of a Ralph Lauren photo shoot for *GQ* or some other high-end publication. Gorgeous men and women sipped drinks and chatted in animated, carefree conversations. Women wore brightly colored dresses and big hats as if they were at the Kentucky Derby, and men donned sport coats and flashy pants I normally only saw in fashion magazines.

Since Porsche was a main sponsor of the Classic, our table was right in front of the horse-jumping action. I said hello to the Porsche dealership owner and his wife and met the others at the table. Heather and I noshed on crab-cake sandwiches and sampled an array of froufrou foods I'd never tasted before. I relished the people watching and enjoyed eating the delicacies.

This is way better than reading People *magazine! This feels like a dream. Thank God Mrs. Newport taught me about etiquette and fine dining.*

Heather was at the event with a friend, who was bold and very excited for us to go meet people and take pictures. If it weren't for her prompting, I don't think I would have met half the people I did that day. When she saw Christie Brinkley, she leaned over to me. "Amy, let's go introduce ourselves and ask if we can get a picture."

"You know what's ironic?" I told her what had happened at Walmart the week before.

"See, it's meant to be. We have to meet her!"

Christie greeted us with a warm smile. She was so sweet. We introduced ourselves, and I told her about the compliment I'd received.

"I can see that," she responded kindly. Bless her heart.

Heather's friend and I also ran into the former mayor of New York City, Rudy Giuliani. I wished him good luck on his campaign, as he was getting ready to run for the presidency. We snapped a quick picture with him and his wife, who was hiding under a wide-brimmed hat.

I gained confidence as we mingled with the crowd. It was a wonderful adventure, and I'm thankful I pushed myself outside my comfort zone. As an added bonus, I also received some amazing goodie bags for me and Eric, filled with high-end facial products and designer fragrances.

I believe God rewarded me that day for having a servant's heart all week. Later, as I sat in the airport and reflected on the experience, Proverbs 22:29 came to mind. "Do you see a [woman] who excels in [her] work? [She] will stand before kings; [she] will not stand before unknown men." I offered a silent prayer of thanks as I boarded the plane heading back to Chicago.

Chapter 42

Speed Bump

Move out of your comfort zone. You can only grow if you are willing to feel awkward and uncomfortable when you try something new.
BRIAN TRACY

"How good are you at roller-skating?" My agent, Ava, asked un-expectedly one afternoon. "And didn't you say your husband is athletic? Can he roller-skate?"

The phone call came while I was catching up at home. I considered the questions. I had taken figure-skating lessons as a kid, and Eric had played hockey. We used to Rollerblade together, and we'd gone roller-skating with youth group and the YMCA teens. Sure, we could skate.

"Great. I have a capital management company that's doing their holiday party downtown. They thought they would spice it up a bit and add some roller-skating waiters, kind of like modern-day carhops. Do you think you could hold a tray of appetizers in one hand while roller-skating around the party, handing them out?"

"I'm always up for a new challenge! Sure, we could do that."

"Great, you'll have lightweight trays and a black leather glove to help hold the tray in place. They'll give you T-shirts with the name of the appetizer you're serving."

A couple of weeks later, Eric and I entered a high-rise building downtown. We were decked out in all black with one leather glove each, prepared to skate the night away. We'd managed to get in one practice session at the local rink to brush up on our skills. I could still skate backward, but my "shoot the duck" was a little rusty.

"Are you ready for this?" I said as we walked toward the party.

"I was born ready," he said to me with a smile.

I felt ready, too, until I saw the ramp we would have to go up and down. "This could get interesting."

"Oh, this is nothing. Just don't dump your tray on me if you fall."

"Yeah, thanks for the vote of confidence."

We met Renee and Steve in our holding area, and the four of us strapped on our skates. We had time to warm up before the partygoers arrived. The event space was rather small and crowded with tables, the bar area, and a DJ booth. And then there was that ramp. It seemed like an obstacle course.

I grabbed a tray, minus the food, and took my first spin around the tables and chairs before the guests arrived. I came near the bar area and said hello to the bartender. As I was looking at him and smiling, my wheels hit a speed bump on the floor, and down I went. Fortunately, I landed on my backside and not my face, and other than the bartender, who stifled a laugh, no one else saw me.

I got up as quickly as possible and took a closer look at what had tripped me. There was a line of electrical cords under a plastic cable protector that ran from the tables over to the bar. It blended in with the floor, and I hadn't noticed it.

"One and done," I told the bartender with a half-smile as I got up off the floor. "That was the first and last fall of the evening."

Those words proved true. Once the guests arrived and music and energy filled the air, we all skated with grace and only an occasional slight bobble. We even managed the ramp. We rolled around tables, chairs, shoe-clad cocktail servers, guests, displays, and more. We served chicken kabobs, lobster rolls, stuffed mushrooms, and a wide array of delicacies.

It turned out to be a memorable date night with Eric and a fabulous way to earn some extra money for the holidays. We even got paid that night, which sweetened the deal. God always seemed to know when Eric and I needed some extra time together, and He was always faithful to provide when we needed it most.

Chapter 43

Future Diplomat

Enjoy the little things in life, because one day you will look back and realize they were the big things.
ROBERT BRAULT

Work ramped up early in January 2008. I finished an auto show in Charleston, West Virginia, went home for a day to repack and see my family, then headed out for another long stretch, beginning in Washington, DC. Thankfully, Eric and Arianna would be joining me for a couple of days in DC. We planned to visit Eric's cousin, Michelle, and do some sightseeing around the nation's capital. We also planned to reconnect with an old friend, a Porsche dealer named Walter.

But just as I was about to enter my room, my agent called. "I know you just arrived and that you're going out to dinner with Trevor and the girls, but you also have to take the Porsche heritage test in the next two days."

I swallowed hard. I'd known I would have to take this test, but I hadn't known the deadline would be this soon. The heritage test was much longer than the monthly test, and I'd have to squeeze it in around getting everything set up for the show, working the booth, and going to this mandatory dinner. *How can I get everything done on time?*

My agent continued. "I know you have a lot to do, but you can't put this off. Do whatever it takes to finish it by Wednesday."

"Okay, I'll do my best."

I came back from dinner late that night feeling exhausted, and I had to be at the convention center early the next morning for the stand turnover with the exhibit company. The lead product specialist was responsible for going in early the first day of an auto show to meet the contact who had set up the booth. The contact would go over all the details before turning the booth over to the product specialist—me. I felt the squeeze on every side.

At the end of the first day of the show, I came back to my room and began the fifty-question test, even though I didn't feel fully prepared. I'd gone through the mandatory study modules Porsche provided the week before in West Virginia, but I still felt overwhelmed by the amount of information. The company let us look up information online as we took the test, but that research could be time consuming. The test could potentially take hours.

And then I remembered the dealers I'd met the week before in West Virginia. They'd given me a sheet of paper with the answers to the test. Although I knew it was okay to ask a dealer or fellow product specialist for help if I was stuck on a particular question, it seemed like quite another thing to fill in a whole list of answers that someone had given me.

In the end, I made the reluctant decision to use the sheet the dealers gave me to complete my test as quickly as possible. It was a decision I questioned then and completely regretted later.

The next day, Sian, a fellow product specialist asked me, "How did you get that test done so fast and do so well?"

"I don't know," I said with a pang of regret welling up in my chest. I didn't want to tell her the truth, and I didn't want to lie. The whole thing made me feel sick to my stomach. I went back to the hotel room that night and cried. I knew I had made the wrong decision. I just wanted to please everyone, cover myself, and ace the test. But the reality was that I'd cheated. The pressures of the job, the travel, and being away from home were coming to a breaking point.

(As a side note, a little over a year later, Eric and I were in a small group at our church. We were studying honesty, and I confessed my Porsche test experience to the other two couples. Our leader, Bob, and the rest of the group encouraged me to reach out to my contacts at Porsche to apologize. I followed their advice and emailed Lee, Trevor, and Phillip a confession and an apology. It was well received, and I felt the shame and guilt lift off of me. It's never too late to make it right!)

I was looking forward to Eric and Arianna's arrival, but when they arrived, our daughter was extremely crabby. She was almost three, and she seemed to be coming down with another cold due to the combination of flying, lack of napping, and the bitter cold weather. We were living at full throttle and asking our daughter to do the same. That night we opted to have dinner at the hotel and go to bed early.

On the following day after work, Carrie made the arrangements for us to meet Walter at the Blair House, the guest house where foreign dignitaries stay when they visit the White House and also where the incoming president stays right before his inauguration. We all had to give our personal information and clear background checks in order to be allowed in the Blair House.

We met up with Walter the next morning on the busy street corner, and I thought he looked like a CIA operative. He wore a dark suit and gray trench coat, and he had black horn-rimmed glasses. He met us with a big smile and warm hugs. Carrie and I had met him when we worked the DC show a couple of years before. He had a full-time job with the government, and he sold Porsches on the side. He was a real enthusiast. On top of that, he was German-American, so I was excited to have him meet Eric.

After brief introductions, we made our way into the Victorian structure, where a hospitable crew greeted us. They took our coats and led us on a tour of the upstairs bedrooms and filled us in on the history of Blair House.

"In here we have memorabilia from various presidents and their administrations. This is actually a bed that Abraham Lincoln and his wife slept in." Our tour guide led us to the room next door. "And this is the guest room where Tony Blair and his wife recently stayed during their visit."

I whispered to Eric, "Where's Arianna?"

"I don't know. She was just here. Let me go look around."

We retraced our steps with Carrie and Walter.

"I found her," Eric said, just loud enough for me to hear. I followed his voice to the bedroom we'd just visited and found Arianna gleefully jumping on the bed.

The bed Lincoln slept in.

I was mortified, and Eric's face was bright red. "Arianna, get down right now! No jumping on the bed!"

Walter chuckled, and his face lit up with a bright smile. "It's okay, she's just a child. This bed has been around for over a hundred years. I think it's stood the test of time. And I enjoy having Arianna here."

"I think she's enjoying it too," I said gratefully. "I'm sorry. She just has so much energy these days."

Arianna was bouncing all over the place. She wanted to run down the hall and explore every nook and cranny. I wished she was still small enough for the teddy bear backpack with the leash.

"Why don't we head downstairs?" Our tour guide said smoothly. "I'll take you to the kitchen and introduce you to the chef. He's preparing a sumptuous dinner for our guests this evening who are visiting from Ireland."

The chef welcomed us warmly and told us about every course he was preparing for the Irish delegates that evening. He even gave us some truffles to sample.

I couldn't get over how welcoming the Blair House was. Maids walked around in black uniforms with white aprons and their hair tucked neatly under white caps. They always stopped what they were doing to greet us when we passed. Being there filled me with a fresh spirit of patriotism. These people made a great first impression for our president and our country.

In the dining room, the tour guide showed us the tables set with white linen and beautiful china. Crystal chandeliers hung from the ceiling. At the front of the room was a podium.

"Go up there with her, and I'll take a picture," Eric said to me.

I carried Arianna up to the podium, and just as I smiled for the camera, she bent down and said, "Hello, I'm Arianna," into the live microphone. Her small, sweet voice carried across the room like a gentle breeze.

"Aww, will you look at that?" Carrie said. "Not even three yet, and she is already speaking at the Blair House."

"Before you all leave," Walter piped in, "I have a gift for Arianna." He handed her a small, soft bag that had a world map on it. It was filled with goodies. "This is what they give each child who visits the Blair House. Everything in it is made in the USA."

We finished up our tour, and Walter drove us back to the hotel. As we were pulling up, he told us, "I have another surprise for you. If you're available, I'd like to take you to the Army Navy Country Club for dinner tomorrow night."

Carrie had to work, but as promised, Walter took Eric, Arianna, and me out again, and we were fortunate to see Washington behind the scenes as we dined at the private club.

Later that week we also had a pleasant dinner with Eric's cousin, Michelle. It was fun to introduce Arianna to people and to see their eyes light up at her silly antics and well-spoken nature. She was a joy to have around most of the time.

Toward the end of their visit, Eric and Arianna stopped by the auto show to see me in the Porsche booth. I took pictures with her and put her in one of the open vehicles so she could "drive." After they left, one of the Porsche dealers said, "I saw you with your husband and your child. I can't believe you're married with a family, and you're still traveling with the auto show. You're a rare breed in this business."

His comments resonated in my mind long after he spoke them. I was coming to the end of four years traveling with Porsche, and maybe it was time to get off the road. I wanted to take care of Arianna, tuck her in at night, and take her to preschool and dance lessons. And I was also thinking about expanding our family.

Three more months and the season would be over. What did I plan to do with my future? I needed to pray and figure out what would be best for me and our family.

Chapter 44

Close to the End

Note to self:
None of us are getting out of here alive, so please stop
treating yourself like an afterthought. Eat the delicious food.
Walk in the sunshine. Jump in the ocean. Say the truth that
you're carrying in your heart like hidden treasure. Be silly.
Be kind. Be weird. There's no time for anything else.
NANEA HOFFMAN

I was burning the candle at both ends. I was traveling all over
the United States and Canada while also auditioning and doing modeling
jobs in Chicago. The travel and long hours were taking a toll on my body.
My cycle was out of whack, and I felt depleted. I couldn't remember the
last time I'd had a full weekend off or when I had last rested.

One day my friend Melanie called and offered Eric and me a job
together. Melanie and I had worked at Porsche together, and now she
had her own modeling agency. I welcomed a job I could do with my
husband and close to home.

On the morning of the event, we drove down to a mall in the southwest suburbs of Chicago. We'd be doing a cell phone promotion for T-Mobile. Eric wore a giant cell phone costume, and I was his handler. I enjoyed working with him as it gave us time to reconnect.

On the way home, I mentioned the pain I'd been experiencing recently. "There's cramping in my uterus, and it's getting worse. It's really low on the right side."

"Well, we have two more days on this job," said Eric. "Why don't you call and make a doctor's appointment for your next day off?"

It made sense. But the pain intensified into the morning. As we drove to our job, it almost became more than I could bear.

"Eric, this is really bad. I took ibuprofen, but I think I should call the OB-GYN."

"Sure, see what they say."

I called the doctor's office and described my symptoms.

"Well, it could be a number of things," said the nurse. "I think you should get checked out right away."

"But I'm on my way to a job. I'm an independent contractor, and we don't have benefits and we don't have sick days. I never call off. I can lose my job and future jobs."

The nurse interrupted. "I understand, and I'm sorry you don't get sick days. But what if this is your appendix rupturing? You could end up in a worse predicament, or you could lose your life. Then you won't need your job, will you?"

In the almost nine years I had worked in the modeling industry, I had only called off from a job one other time. I worked while sick, with laryngitis, with food poisoning, while hiding a pregnancy, and with morning sickness. This time it was different.

"Yeah, you scared me straight. What do you suggest I do?"

"Get to the ER now. Do you have someone who can drive you?"

"Yes, my husband can drop me off at the hospital before he goes to work."

"Smart choice. I wish you the best, and I think you're doing the right thing."

"Thank you." I hung up the phone and looked at Eric. "Well, Mr. Cell-Phone Man, I can't be there today. You're going to have to find a new handler."

Later, as I sat in the ER waiting room consumed with worry, I looked up to find Eric's Aunt Cindy. She worked at the hospital and happened to be on shift while I was there.

She gave me a big hug. "I'll pray for you. I know this is scary, but you're in good hands."

The nurses and techs ran test after test on me that day, and everything came up inconclusive. The pain wasn't my appendix, kidney stones, gallstones, or a number of other things. I had X-rays, blood tests, and an ultrasound. They all came back normal.

Finally, the hospital sent me home, telling me I should make an appointment with the OB-GYN and have some further testing done there.

I knew the pain wasn't just in my head. I couldn't shake the fear of the unknown that was crushing in on me. I called Jeri, and she picked me up and drove me home to Huntley.

"Maybe I have cancer or some sort of disease," I fretted. "But I don't feel that sick."

"I think you just need to go home and rest," said Jeri. "Take a nap and let Eric get Arianna from the sitter after work. Your body is telling you to rest. And then make an appointment with the OB as soon as you can, so you can put your mind at ease."

I took Jeri's advice, letting myself into my empty house and plopping down on the couch. I cozied up in some blankets but still felt restless. I poured my heart out to God. I pleaded with Him to make me well so I could be there for Arianna and Eric. I promised to slow down and work less. I prayed I didn't have some life-threatening disease. The whole episode was like a wake-up call, and it certainly got my attention.

I returned to work the next day after filling Melanie in on what had happened. The day after that, I sat in my OB-GYN's office hoping for some answers.

The nurse did an internal ultrasound on me. She didn't say too much, but a few minutes later, the doctor came in.

"You have a ruptured cyst on your ovary. These can be extremely painful, and I'm not surprised you ended up in the ER. It's a slow rupture, which is why the pain is lasting so long. The good news is that because it's already ruptured, we don't have to go in and remove it. We need to just let it run its course."

"What a relief! I thought I had some terminal illness. My life has been crazy busy . . ." I told the doctor about my hectic work schedule.

"You're doing way too much. Your body is telling you to rest," the doctor told me as she pulled out her notepad. "You need a vacation. I don't do this very often, but I'm writing you a prescription for a vacation. Doctor's orders." She smiled as she handed me the small slip of paper. "And I mean it. Your life and your health depend on it."

Well, that was certainly a firm mandate. My mind started to race. *How can we afford a vacation? We're trying to get Eric through DePaul, and we just enrolled Arianna in dance lessons. We have to pay for preschool, and we're coming into a slow season for my work. We need to save. How can we do this?*

After sharing the news with Eric, we brainstormed affordable vacations. We decided to go to Mesa, Arizona, to visit my parents who spent their winters there. My mom had been battling uterine cancer, and I thought she would like to spend some extra time with us after her surgery. We booked our airline tickets and talked about taking a side trip to Sedona.

Before we could go, though, I had more work to do. The pain slowly subsided, but it took a couple of weeks to fully recover. My energy was depleted for a time, but I trudged forward.

I flew out to Denver in the middle of March for a charity event that Porsche was cosponsoring with the local major sports teams. Alexandra, or Alex, the other product specialist, and I made our way to the Pepsi Center, where we met Heather from Porsche Cars North America to get our assignments for the evening.

I stood on the basketball court that night near one of the Porsche 911s, explaining the car's specs to different athletes and invited guests and inviting them to hop in the car and check it out.

A very tall basketball player from the Nuggets approached, and I encouraged him to sit in the car. He had to be nearly seven feet tall, but he managed to squeeze his lanky frame into the small sports car. As I showed him how to adjust the seat, we were bathed in a bright light, and I realized a TV news crew had come to capture our interaction. The player crammed his legs in, but they hit the steering wheel. We both laughed as I told him about the car.

"You know, you can customize the vehicle as well as the seat. You can have it lowered by two centimeters to help accommodate your height."

He shook his head. "I think Porsche is a sweet ride. I just don't know if I can fit in here."

"Well, there is always the Cayenne, our SUV, and we are coming out with Panamera, a four-door sedan, soon."

The entire event space was filled with people. Music echoed through the arena, Allen Iverson was bartending, and the atmosphere was charged with electricity. Athletes mingled with guests, and everyone ate appetizers, sipped on drinks, danced, and played basketball.

As things were wrapping up, Heather mentioned that she wanted to go out afterward. I was exhausted from my travels and health condition.

I just wanted to go back to the hotel and sleep. Yet something inside me told me to go out that night.

We ended up at the hotel right next to the Pepsi Center, and we sat together in the bar. As Heather, Alex, and I talked, it became apparent this was a divine appointment.

Heather asked me, "How are you so positive all the time? I want to know where you get your energy and your strength."

I paused a moment. "Honestly, I believe my strength comes from God. I spend time with Him every day through reading my Bible and prayer. I get encouragement from Him and wisdom to know how to handle things."

"Wow, that's really cool. How did that all come about?"

I explained how, when I was at Auburn, I'd met a Christian named Annie. She befriended me, and we hung out together a lot. Annie told me about Jesus and how I could have a personal relationship with Him. "She told me it wasn't just about religion or doing the right thing, but about inviting Jesus to live in my heart and getting to know God through Him. That's how it all started."

"That's cool, Amy."

Alex was a devout Mormon, and she shared more about her beliefs as well. She was a very grounded person, and I admired her humility, work ethic, and strong morals.

As the evening was ending, I told my friends, "One of my favorite verses is in Jeremiah 29:11. It says, 'I know the plans I have for you, plans to prosper you and not to harm you. To give you a future and a hope.' Jesus is just a prayer away."

Heather said, "Amy and Alex, I'm so glad I got to talk to both of you tonight. I really needed this. Thank you for always going above and beyond for Porsche. We appreciate all that you do. You ladies are amazing."

And with that, we said good night and made our way back to our hotel. The conversation had lasted into the early morning hours, but God gave me the strength to get through it. I whispered a prayer of thanks for the opportunity and a prayer for Heather, that she would come to know Jesus and His love for her. I felt refreshed and encouraged by our conversation as I realized that God truly orchestrates everything in our lives so perfectly.

Chapter 45

Change on the Horizon

Change is hard at first, messy in the middle, and gorgeous at the end.
ROBIN SHARMA

My contract with Porsche was coming to an end. I had one final auto show booked in Vancouver, British Columbia, and then Eric and I were going on vacation.

One Sunday, as we were driving home from church, Arianna piped up from the backseat. "When am I going to get a little brother or sister?"

"Well, Dad and I have actually been praying about that very thing. We're trying to decide when the time is right to have another baby, and we're asking God what He thinks."

She was quiet for a few seconds. "Mom, Dad, God said yes."

I laughed and looked at Eric. "Well, it looks like we have our answer. We have a thumbs-up from Arianna and apparently God too."

Eric smiled. "Maybe we should try soon."

I felt hope rise in my spirit. *If I walk away from Porsche, it would be wonderful to get pregnant and have a baby boy.*

Not long after that, I sat relaxing in the sun and breathing in the fresh air of the Pacific Northwest. There's something to be said for the breeze off the Pacific Ocean and the air quality in that region. I always feel better and sleep better there. Plus, Vancouver is quite the experience with its breathtaking views, quaint restaurants and shops, ethnic diversity, and delicious food. They were preparing for the 2010 Olympic games. A buzz filled the air.

Eric's friend Jared's parents were missionaries there and would be picking me up after the auto show. They were going to give me a tour of their home and the Dream Center, their outreach to the people of Vancouver, and then take me out for dinner in the city. I was looking forward to some encouraging time with friends.

We sat down at a hip restaurant later that evening, and I shared my heart with the Johnsons. "I feel like God is taking us somewhere new. Eric's parents have helped us so much, but I feel like God is saying it's time to fly on our own. We've been praying, and we're going to check out the possibility of moving to Colorado Springs. We've also been talking about expanding our family, and I'm planning to leave Porsche after this season."

Mrs. Johnson responded, "It sounds like you have a lot of exciting changes coming soon. God is always faithful to order our steps, one at a time."

"Yes, He is. I keep seeing a vision of Eric and me as two baby birds in a nest. We're on the edge, getting ready to jump out and fly."

"That can be exciting and scary at the same time," Mr. Johnson added. "It's a lot like being a missionary. You go where He leads, and you trust that He will be with you and provide for you each step of the way."

During the flight home, I reflected on my trip. It had been my last auto show for Porsche. I smiled as I scrolled through the pictures on my phone.

God had taken me and my family to some amazing places. I thought about all the travel and the fabulous sights we'd seen and the many people we'd met. I let out a long sigh and felt my heart swell with gratitude for all the good things He had done for me and for my family.

When I graduated from modeling school in 1999, Eric and I had walked around downtown Chicago, dreaming about where a career in modeling might take me. I had questioned how much or how far I could go. But God took me farther than I expected and opened doors I couldn't even have imagined then. He had called me to be a pioneer and to blaze a trail. He had promised He would show up, and He certainly did. Even in those early years when I questioned whether I'd made the right decision, He kept showing Himself faithful, I kept stepping out, and He kept keeping His promise.

Now, as I reminisced, I felt a sense of complete fulfillment. Mission accomplished.

I was at a fork in the road. One path beckoned me to my career. I had favor with Porsche, and I dreamed of racing. I could hear Bill, our Porsche trainer, saying, "Stick with us, Amy, and we'll teach you how to race."

And yet as I pondered the other path, the path of family and motherhood, it seemed so inviting. This hadn't been my strong suit to date. I didn't feel overly maternal, I couldn't cook to save my life, and I didn't enjoy crafting or doing girlie things. And yet deep inside, I longed to be home with my daughter, to snuggle her every morning and tuck her in every night. I wanted to take her to the local park and scale the jungle gym with her. I wanted to be the person raising her. I could still hear Arianna's little voice as she'd said to me once as I prepared to go on another trip, "You know, I have another mom." It broke my heart every time I thought of it.

As I prayed on the airplane, I handed it all over to God. My Porsche job, my dreams of racing, my modeling, and my desire to write and speak one day. It's as if I saw it all being put on the back burner of a stove. On the front burner were Arianna and Eric. I wanted to support Eric as he sought to become the main provider. I wanted to try for another child. I wanted to find modeling jobs closer to home that worked well for my family. Chicago had lots of trade shows, and while they weren't as exciting and glamorous as other modeling work, they were direct bookings (no need to audition), and they paid well.

I knew my agent would call at the end of the month and ask me to return to Porsche for the 2008–2009 season, and I knew my answer would be no. That meant I wouldn't get summer work from them either. But the winds of change were blowing through, and a new season was upon us.

As I continued to scroll through my pictures, tears welled up in my eyes. I realized how privileged I had been on this journey. God had honored my tiny steps of faith so many years ago, and He'd done much more than I ever expected.

God, if this is all You ever do for me in this lifetime, I am blessed beyond my wildest dreams. Thank You so much for everything. I commit my life to You, and I trust this next season to You, wherever You take me and my family.

Chapter 46

A New Path

To become "unique," the challenge is to fight the hardest battle which anyone can imagine until you reach your destination.
A. P. J. Abdul Kalam

I had no clue on that plane ride home from Vancouver how drastically our lives would change over the next couple of years. I continued to model and work, and then, on May 11, 2009, I gave birth to a baby boy. Ashton David Tyler came into our lives and rocked our world. Ashton was a planned C-section and, just like his sister, was born breach.

Eric chuckled when he said, "Amy, our kids like to come running into the world." I took solace from the words of the anesthesiologist: "Mom, you know what that means? If a child is born breach, he is really smart." I think both of those descriptions are pretty fitting for our children.

But Ashton had swallowed meconium during the delivery and was whisked away to the neonatal intensive care unit (NICU) moments after his birth. Nine days and a slew of tests later, we learned he had multiple health issues. After leaving the NICU, we followed up with a cardiologist, who diagnosed Ashton with an innocent heart murmur and a mild form of pulmonary artery stenosis. We also saw an ear, nose, and throat specialist (ENT) and discovered our baby had laryngomalacia, or a "floppy airway." A visit to the urologist was next on the list, and there we learned Ashton would need surgery to fix some other issues.

Over the next two and a half years, Ashton would spend more time in the hospital, see many specialists, and undergo three surgeries in all. We thought he had overcome these health issues, until we realized at about age six that he wasn't growing at a normal rate. We heard words from the pediatrician like "failure to thrive," as he measured in only the bottom 2 percent on the growth chart.

After a visit with a new pediatric cardiologist, an endocrinologist, and a genetic test, we discovered that all of Ashton's health issues were related. In February of 2017, he was diagnosed with Noonan syndrome, a genetic disorder affecting him at PTPN11. Thankfully, Ashton has the mild form, but the diagnosis brought more specialists and numerous tests into our lives. We began to administer nightly growth hormone injections.

It has been a journey, but we have held on to God's promises for Ashton in Psalm 139:15–17 (NLT): "You watched me as I was being formed in utter seclusion, as I was woven together in the dark of the womb. You saw me before I was born. Every day of my life was recorded in your book. Every moment was laid out before a single day had passed. How precious are your thoughts about me, O God. They cannot be numbered!"

God has shown Himself faithful time and time again over these last ten years. Eric completed his classes at DePaul University a short time after I left Porsche. Before graduating from the School of New Learning (SNL) program there, however, his final project had to be approved by his two advisors and the board. That final project seemed to go on forever, but finally in 2011, Eric gained his advisors' approval, presented it before the board, and passed with flying colors. The project included a paper on how to write a business plan and an actual, full-scale business plan for Automated Lighting Design.

Eric's perseverance was honored in the end, as he not only earned his BA in international business and marketing, but he also received high acclaim. He was told that his project was so well done that it would be used as a template at DePaul's SNL program on how to develop a business plan. He also sat on a panel with his advisors after he graduated to give feedback to underclassmen. And he has even been a guest teacher at DePaul since graduating at the invitation of his former advisor.

At the same time, I was praying for direction about my career and work. One day Ashton and I were at our local library, when my son toddled over to me and handed me a book entitled *Ronald Reagan: My Life at 100*. It had been a while since I had read anything of substance, and I decided this was a sign I should start reading again. While reading, I came up with my next assignment, my own personal Three Rs—reading, running, and (w)riting. Instead of seeking a full-time job or going back to college for my master's degree, I set three goals for myself: I would read a hundred books before Ashton went into kindergarten, I'd write my life story, and I would run another marathon for charity.

The reading part was probably the easiest. I listened to books as I ran and in the car as I commuted to work. I also picked up a book every night before bed. Some of the books that left the greatest impression on me were *Spoken from the Heart*, by Laura Bush; *Decision Points*, by George W. Bush; *How to Get Out of Your Own Way*, by Tyrese Gibson; *Reposition Yourself: Living Life without Limits*, by T. D. Jakes; *The Best Yes*, by Lysa TerKeurst; and *Running for My Life: One Lost Boy's Journey from the Killing Fields of Sudan to the Olympic Games*, by Lopez Lomong.

I started writing my story from beginning to end. I had no training in writing, so I just wrote whatever came to mind. I had met Nicole O'Dell in 2013. We were both speaking at Christian Life College's Ascension Convention that year. She encouraged me to start writing a blog for

Choose Now Ministries. I wrestled with my fear about writing for the public eye, but eventually I took her up on the offer and even started my own email blog. It's taken a few years, but after receiving direction from my friend Debbie Lykins, editorial help and writing techniques from Beth Jusino, and a few life-coaching sessions over the phone from Bob Goff, I shaped my life story into this memoir, and my publisher finished the rest.

In 2013, I tied together my desire to run and my desire to do something significant by running for charity. I decided to run the Walt Disney World Marathon for Team in Training, as I had previously run with them in Alaska in 2005. I ran Disney in 2014 and raised money for the Leukemia & Lymphoma Society. Later that fall, I ran the Bank of America Chicago Marathon with Team World Vision, raising money for clean drinking water in Africa. Unfortunately, I reinjured my back at the end of 2014, but I continued to press on.

Our whole family got involved, and over the next few years, we raised money for Team World Vision and Refuge for Women. Arianna and Ashton have been a fixture on the running trail over the years, cheering on our teams. Arianna was a top fundraiser for Team World Vision in 2016, even though she was only eleven years old and still too young to run the half marathon. We have enjoyed hosting fundraiser breakfasts at our home, and as a family, we have raised almost $20K combined for these charities. In 2017, as Eric and Ashton cheered us on, Arianna and I ran/walked the Crystal Lake Half Marathon together for Team World Vision and crossed the finish line holding hands.

While I have worked to put my family first during this season, I continue to juggle trade shows, occasional modeling jobs and speaking gigs, and of course, my writing. We have been to a lot of doctors and specialists with Ashton but have also made some amazing memories taking day trips to Chicago or road trips to Minnesota and around the country.

We spend a lot of normal days just watching flag football or going to piano lessons, but we have also had some really hard days, cramming in long hours at work, commuting from the city, and taking Ashton for long, hard tests at the hospital. As we moved my career to the back burner and Eric's to the front, I became the primary caregiver for our children. Eric has become the primary breadwinner through his hard work and long hours at Automated Lighting Design.

And now, after seven years in the making, another dream is about to come true with the release of *Model Behavior* in 2019. I have been given so many opportunities and have experienced so many wonderful things, that I can only look forward in anticipation to what God has next in store for me, Eric, and our family. I hope to gain more speaking opportunities, and I plan to continue writing. I believe the best is yet to come!

If I've learned one thing through my adventures, it's that even though we may not accomplish everything on our timetable or in the way we anticipated, we can be encouraged to know that God is always moving behind the scenes. True to His Word, He's working all things together for good and bringing our dreams, visions, and purpose to fruition in His perfect way.

Conclusion

Our deepest fear is not that we are inadequate. Our deepest fear is that we are powerful beyond measure. It is our light, not our darkness, that most frightens us. We ask ourselves, "Who am I to be brilliant, gorgeous, talented, fabulous?" Actually, who are you not to be? Your playing small does not serve the world. There is nothing enlightened about shrinking so that other people won't feel insecure around you. We are all meant to shine, as children do. It's not just in some of us; it's in everyone. And as we let our own light shine, we unconsciously give other people permission to do the same. As we are liberated from our own fear, our presence automatically liberates others.

MARIANNE WILLIAMSON

Dear reader, my hope and prayer is that, as you read this book, you have been encouraged to follow your own dreams and pursue what God has for you, even if you don't feel ready or perfect, and even if you don't have it all figured out. The fact that I started modeling at twenty-nine isn't just rare; it's almost unheard of in the industry. I also was never the skinniest girl, and I have some facial imperfections. But God showed me favor.

I'm so glad I took the advice of Frederic Fekkai, who told me to be myself and to stay natural, and I would do well. He told me I didn't need plastic surgery.

I remember, too, my former youth pastor, Phil Baker, who popped into an Ascension Convention session where I was speaking one year. When he heard my story, Phil also advised me to stay the way I was and let God use the very imperfections I wanted to hide, because I was a testimony of what God can do with a yielded vessel and an imperfect person.

So that's what I did. I renamed my birthmark my blessing. I went into the modeling industry imperfect, worked in the industry imperfect, and continue to do life imperfectly. The only explanation for my success is that God called me to do it, granted me favor, and opened doors. In Zechariah 4:6 (NIV), the Lord says it's "not by might nor by power, but by my Spirit."

Romans 11:29 says, "For the gifts and the calling of God are irrevocable." In other words, He doesn't take them back. God won't change His mind and renege on the offer. You can't make too many mistakes or grow too old or blow it too many times. The gifts and the calling will remain. It is only up to you and me to believe God, believe in ourselves, and move forward into all He has for us.

God loves us too much to force us to do something we don't want to do. He is a perfect gentleman and a patient father. He'll wait for us to make the decision to trust Him and move forward in our gifting.

I prayed hard before every job. I always prayed that my weaknesses and imperfections and even my "blessing" would be swallowed up in His love and grace. I prayed that the love of God would shine through me, and that He would grant me favor. I prayed that all my strengths would show. I always prayed a blessing over the client, the studio, the trade show booth, and the other talent. And I prayed that the companies I worked for would be blessed, that sales would exceed expectation, and that they would grow and prosper.

I often prayed that the people I met would come to a saving faith in Jesus Christ. I prayed that things would go smoothly and easily and effortlessly and that I would be asked back. And I was. I worked a number of print jobs, informal modeling jobs, or character jobs for the same companies, and I was sent to the same trade shows and events for MET-Rx from year to year.

I did my best, and God did the rest. I would pray every day that God's favor would surround me like a shield. Psalm 5:12 (NIV) says, "Surely, Lord, you bless the righteous; you surround them with your favor as with a shield." Proverbs 11:27 promises, "He who earnestly seeks good finds favor."

I think when you invite God in to fill you with His strength, power, wisdom, and favor, it takes the pressure off you. I still did my best and aimed to be a person of excellence on every job, but ultimately, I trusted God to show up and show out.

I hope my story is an inspiration to you. It doesn't matter what your age is, where you grew up, or whether you have the right education. It doesn't matter if you are qualified or physically perfect. Henry Blackaby, author of *Experiencing God*, has said, "The reality is that the Lord never calls the qualified; He qualifies the called." Our only job is to surrender to God and to invite Him to come in and make a path for us. If the path is not clearly marked, together you and God can forge a new one. And when the path becomes dark, scary, and uncertain at times, you can still be assured that God is there with you, and He will lead you through.

Psalm 16:11 says, "You will show me the path of life; in Your presence is fullness of joy; at Your right hand are pleasures forevermore." My encouragement to you is, *go for it*! What are you waiting for? I believe God has amazing experiences in store for you!

Order Information

REDEMPTION PRESS

To order additional copies of this book, please visit
www.redemption-press.com.
Also available on Amazon.com and BarnesandNoble.com
Or by calling toll free 1-844-2REDEEM.

CPSIA information can be obtained
at www.ICGtesting.com
Printed in the USA
FFHW022207050319
50862243-56261FF